THE AMERICAN NEGRO

HIS HISTORY AND LITERATURE

NEGRO PROTEST PAMPHLETS

A Compendium

ARNO PRESS and THE NEW YORK TIMES

NEW YORK 1969

General Editor
WILLIAM LOREN KATZ

Long before the Civil War, black men who were denied redress of their grievances in the courts or in state legislatures frequently had recourse to various literary means of publicizing their grievances or stating their protests. These written protests concerned the diversified themes of slavery and its abolition, the education of blacks and their rights to moral and religious freedom, occupations of black people and their right to be compensated for their labor, and a host of other issues. In this way a considerable body of protest literature was accumulated.

Predominantly the vogue among black writers, the pamphlet form was sustained by black preachers who evidently found its slender format no incumbrance to their desires to reach beyond their immediate congregations to all those unnumbered blacks who were thought to be able to read. Clearly, the pamphlet writers realized that the words of ministers were a sure way of reaching and swaying not only their fellow blacks, but such sympathetic whites as might lend an ear, as well as monetary assistance, to the cause which they advocated.

As the several addresses and polemical statements here presented will show, church meetings, conventions, and other assemblies were often occasions for vehement exposure of social injustice. As one might suppose, these gatherings were usually held in church buildings, which afforded the incumbent pastor or church leader an opii

portunity to express himself fully in opposition to the
oppressive social conditions that were the subject of the
occasion. The publication of actions taken or issues dis-
cussed in such meetings helped to swell the tide of pamphlet literature in those early times.

The first of the protests in this volume is a rebuttal to
an unfair, or, probably, a prejudiced judgment by Matthew Carey, a Philadelphia publicist, on the motives and
character of certain Negroes of that city at the time of
the yellow fever epidemic in 1793. Carey, in his account
of the epidemic, said that some of the Negroes who were
helping the victims had been "detected in plundering."
However, Carey complimented Absalom Jones, Richard
Allen, and Thomas Gray, the Negro leaders, saying they
should receive "public gratitude" for their efforts. Jones
and Allen retorted that the charges against the black persons they had directed in combating the plague vitiated
Carey's praise, and quickly collaborated on this well-
organized, objective, and forceful refutation.

Included in this pamphlet is a markedly direct, though
short and temperate, "Address to Those Who Keep Slaves
and Approve the Practice," which was probably written
by Richard Allen alone. The author assumed that those
to whom he addressed his appeal were cognizant of the
Old Testament history of the Hebrews, and he therefore
relied heavily on scriptural authority in his appeal to the
conscience and to the "just reason" with which he apparently credits the slaveholder.

Daniel Coker, in his *A Dialogue Between a Virginian
and an African Minister*, likewise depends on biblical
authority, in a way that is both elaborate and pedantic.
Coker's arguments against slavery and its concomitant
evils is couched in the form of scholastic or Socratic dialogue, and is sprinkled quite liberally with phrases seem-
ingly derived from a familiarity with legal discourse. In
addition to his proved abilities as an organizer of Negroes
for Methodism, Coker shared Allen's enthusiasm for the

establishment of a separate African Methodist Church. Indeed, had the times so directed, he might have become the effective leader of African Methodism. However, he left America in 1820 in the company of a band of emigrants to Liberia, and subsequently built a church in Sierra Leone.

Nathaniel Paul, whose eloquent *An Address Delivered on the Celebration of the Abolition of Slavery in the State of New York*, recalls more the declamatory style of the English parliamentarian of his day than it does the turgid eloquence of the Afro-American preacher, was well chosen to descant upon the abolition of slavery in New York by the legislature of that state. His address recounts the iniquities produced in society by human slavery and concludes with a reasoned, clear-sighted, and statesman-like appraisal of the social and educational advantages that are to be drawn from the freedoms that, by legislative enactment, have been placed within the black man's reach and grasp.

This remarkable address impales the "palpable inconsistencies [of social and political custom] which abound in America," and thereby finds both spiritual and tactical extension in William Hamilton's *Address to the Fourth Annual Convention of the People of Color of the United States*. Hamilton, anticipating by many years Abraham Lincoln's "house divided" speech, characterizes American society of his day as "a community of castes with separate interests" and asserts that reason has not full sway "until the community shall see that a wrong done to one is a wrong done to the whole." He brands the Colonialization Society and its work as "Devil's allure" and as a source of possibly fatal division among the people of color, for its advocacy of expatriation in Africa rather than the pursuit of freedom at home.

The stigma of racial inferiority, which the supporters of the slavocracy imputed to black seeker's of freedom, was necessarily assailed by all those who clung to the possibility of American citizenship, such as the Reverend Hosea Easton, a self-styled "colored man." His *A Treatise on the Intellectual Character and Civil and Political Condition of the Colored People of the United States* is an impressive assault against spurious charges of racial inferiority. In significant detail the author brings all such charges before the bar of history, and by tabular juxtaposition, seeks to prove that the biblical descent of the European nations from the stem of Japeth has led to barbarism and the bloody disasters of insensate national strife; while the descendents of Ham, the accursed of Noah, eschewing both war and slavery, have chosen to guide humanity in the arts of peace.

In his discussion of the civil and political condition of his people, the Reverend Easton's insistence on the early and indisputable "claims of the colored subjects of this government to equal political rights" is certainly interesting, and must have seemed challenging in his day. In this connection his protest attaches to the principle that "the colored people" were, like other Americans, entitled to the freedoms of independent statehood that had been won by the American Revolution. Arguments in support of this principle are cited by Easton from speeches made by such patriots as Richard Henry Lee, and from the Declaration of Independence, the Articles of Confederation, from customary law, and, most effectively of all, from the recorded acknowledgment of participation by Negroes in the American Revolution and subsequent wars. It is ironical, in the light of his disclosures, that the black American of the present century has had to insist upon his rights to military service and rank in both World Wars.

As anyone knows who has some acquaintance with the history of military service by Negroes on the side of the Union during the Civil War, the first official northern contingent of black soldiers in that war marched under the banner of the Fifty-fourth Massachusetts Regiment. In the light of that fact, the impassioned plea for an independent military company, made by William J. Watkins in 1853 before the State Legislative Committee on the Militia at Boston might be described as a portent of things to come. Watkins' petition was a test of legislative sentiment in Massachusetts toward the rights of black men to bear arms in the defense of their state and country, and toward their desire to be grouped together as a single military unit (composed of blacks alone) which might be incorporated into the national militia in time of crisis. The petition presented by Watkins bore the signatures of sixty-five black men, a number of whom were said by Watkins to be "descendents of revolution sires, and revolution mothers" whose "blood flowed freely in defence of their country . . . and who died that we might live as Freemen."

Although the language of these very significant documents may at times be high-flown, they are, nevertheless, statements that clearly denote the determination of blacks, in times prior to the Civil War, to lay claim to unrestricted civil and political rights in every area of American life and responsible citizenship.

Dorothy Porter
CURATOR, MOORLAND-SPINGARN COLLECTION
HOWARD UNIVERSITY

THE PAMPHLETS

ABSALOM JONES AND RICHARD ALLEN

*A Narrative of the Proceedings
of the Black People, During the Late Awful Calamity
in Philadelphia, in the Year, 1793*

DANIEL COKER

*A Dialogue Between a Virginian
and an African Minister*

NATHANIEL PAUL

*An Address, Delivered on the Celebration
of the Abolition of Slavery,
in the State of New York, July 5, 1827*

WILLIAM HAMILTON

*Address to the Fourth Annual Convention
of the People of Color of the United States*

HOSEA EASTON

*A Treatise on the Intellectual Character,
and Civil and Political Condition
of the Colored People of the United States*

WILLIAM J. WATKINS

*Our Rights as Men. An Address Delivered in Boston,
Before the Legislative Committee on the Militia,
February 24, 1853*

ABSALOM JONES AND RICHARD ALLEN

A Narrative of the Proceedings
of the Black People, During the Late Awful Calamity
in Philadelphia, in the Year, 1793

A

NARRATIVE

OF THE

PROCEEDINGS

OF THE

Black People,

DURING THE LATE

AWFUL CALAMITY IN PHILADELPHIA,

IN THE YEAR, 1793:

AND A

REFUTATION

OF SOME

CENSURES,

THROWN UPON THEM IN SOME LATE PUBLICATIONS.

BY A. J. AND R. A.

PHILADELPHIA: PRINTED FOR THE AUTHORS.

LONDON:
RE-PRINTED, AND SOLD BY DARTON AND HARVEY.
NO. 55, GRACECHURCH-STREET.

1794.

PRICE THREEPENCE.

A

NARRATIVE, &c.

IN confequence of a partial reprefentation of the conduct of the people who were employed to nurfe the fick, in the late calamitous ftate of the city of Philadelphia, we are folicited, by a number of thofe who feel themfelves injured thereby, and by the advice of feveral refpectable citizens, to ftep forward and declare facts as they really were; feeing that from our fituation, on account of the charge we took upon us, we had it more fully and generally in our power, to know and obferve the conduct and behaviour of thofe that were fo employed.

Early in September, a folicitation appeared in the public papers, to the people of colour to come forward and affift the diftreffed, perifhing, and neglected fick; with a kind of affurance, that people of our colour were not liable to take the infection. Upon which we and a few others met and confulted how to act on fo truly alarming and melancholy an occafion. After fome converfation, we found a freedom to go forth, confiding in him who can preferve in the midft of a burning fiery furnace, fenfible that it was our duty to do all the good we could to our fuffering fellow mortals. We fet out to fee where we could be ufeful. The firft we vifited was a man in Emfley's-Alley, who was dying, and his wife lay dead at the time in the houfe, there were none to affift but two poor helplefs children. We adminiftered what relief we could, and applied to the overfeers of the poor to have the woman buried. We vifited upwards of twenty families that day—they were fcenes of woe indeed! The Lord was pleafed to ftrengthen us, and remove all fear from us, and difpofed our hearts to be as ufeful as poffible.

In

In order the better to regulate our conduct, we called on the mayor next day, to confult with him how to proceed, fo as to be moft ufeful. The firft object he recommended was a ftrict attention to the fick, and the procuring of nurfes. This was attended to by Abfalom Jones and William Gray; and, in order that the diftreffed might know where to apply, the mayor advertifed the public that upon application to them they would be fupplied. Soon after, the mortality increafing, the difficulty of getting a corpfe taken away, was fuch, that few were willing to do it, when offered great rewards. The black people were looked to. We then offered our fervices in the publicpapers, by advertifing that we would remove the dead and procure nurfes. Our fervices were the production of real fenfibility;— we fought not fee nor reward, until the increafe of the diforder rendered our labour fo arduous that we were not adequate to the fervice we had affumed. The mortality increafing rapidly, obliged us to call in the affiftance of five * hired men, in the awful difcharge of interring the dead. They, with great reluctance, were prevailed upon to join us. It was very uncommon, at this time, to find any one that would go near, much more, handle, a fick or dead perfon.

Mr. Carey, in page 106 of his third edition, has obferved, that, " for the honor of human nature, it ought to be recorded, that fome of the convicts in the gaol, a part of the term of whofe confinement had been remitted as a reward for their peaceable, orderly behaviour, voluntarily offered themfelves as nurfes to attend the fick at Bufh-hill; and have, in that capacity, conducted themfelves with great fidelity, &c". Here it ought to be remarked, (although Mr. Carey hath not done it) that two thirds of the perfons, who rendered thefe effential fervices, were people of colour, who, on the application of the elders of the African church, (who met to confider what they could do for the help of the fick) were liberated, on condition of their doing the duty of nurfes at the hofpital at Bufh-hill; which they as voluntarily accepted to do, as they did faithfully difcharge, this fevere and difagreeable duty.—May the Lord reward them, both temporally and fpiritually.

* Two of whom were Richard Allen's brothers.

When

When the ficknefs became general, and feveral of the phyfi-
cians died, and moft of the furvivors were exhaufted by ficknefs or fatigue; that good man, Dr. Rufh, called us more immediately to attend upon the fick, knowing we could both
bleed; he told us we could increafe our utility, by attending to
his inftructions, and accordingly directed us where to procure
medicine duly prepared, with proper direction, how to adminif-
ter them, and at what ftages of the diforder to bleed; and when
we found ourfelves incapable of judging what was proper to be
done, to apply to him, and he would, if able, attend them himfelf, or fend Edward Fifher, his pupil, which he often did;
and Mr. Fifher manifefted his humanity, by an affectionate attention for their relief.—This has been no fmall fatisfaction to
us; for, we think, that when a phyfician was not attainable, we
have been the inftruments, in the hand of God, for faving the
lives of fome hundreds of our fuffering fellow mortals.

We feel ourfelves fenfibly aggrieved by the cenforious epithets
of many, who did not render the leaft affiftance in the time of
neceffity, yet are liberal of their cenfure of us, for the prices
paid for our fervices, when no one knew how to make a propo-
fal to any one they wanted to affift them. At firft we made no
charge, but left it to thofe we ferved in removing their dead,
to give what they thought fit—we fet no price, until the reward
was fixed by thofe we had ferved. After paying the people we
had to affift us, our compenfation is much lefs than many will
believe.

We do affure the public, that *all* the money we have received
for burying, and for coffins which we ourfelves purchafed and
procured, has not defrayed the expence of wages which we had
to pay to thofe whom we employed to affift us. The following
ftatement is accurately made:

CASH RECEIVED.

The whole amount of Cafh we received for burying the dead, and for burying beds, is,   £. 233 10 4

CASH PAID.

For coffins, for which we have received nothing - - - - £. 33 0 0

Carry over £. 33 0 0

A 3

Brought

Brought forward   £. 33   o   o
For the hire of five men, 3 of
  them 70 days each, and the
  other two, 63 days each, at
  22/6 per day, - - - - - 378   o   o
                 411   o   o

Debts due us, for which we expect but little
     £.110   o   o
From this ftatement, for the truth of which we
folemnly vouch, it is evident, and we fenfibly feel the operation of the fact, that we are
out of pocket, - - - - - -   £.177   9   8

Befides the cofts of hearfes, the maintenance of our families
for 70 days, (being the period of our labours) and the fupport
of the five hired men, during the refpective times of their being employed ; which expences, together with fundry gifts we
occafionally made to poor families, might reafonably and properly be introduced, to fhew our actual fituation with regard to
profit—but it is enough to exhibit to the public, from the above
fpecified items, of *Cafb paid, and Cafb received*, without taking
into view the other expences, that, by the employment we were
engaged in, we have loft £. 177 9 8. But, if the other expences, which we have actually paid, are added to that fum,
how much then may we not fay we have fuffered ! We leave the
public to judge.

It may poffibly appear ftrange to fome who know how con-
ftantly we were employed, that we fhould have received no
more Cafh than £.233 10 4. But we repeat our affurance,
that this is the fact, and we add another, will ferve the better to
explain it : We have buried *feveral hundreds* of poor perfons
and ftrangers, for which fervice we have never received, nor
never afked any compenfation.

We feel ourfelves hurt moft by a partial, cenforious paragraph, in Mr. Carey's fecond edition, of his account of the
ficknefs, &c. in Philadelphia ; pages 76 and 77, where he af-
perfes the blacks alone, for having taken the advantage of the
diftreffed fituation of the people. That fome extravagant prices
were paid, we admit ; but how came they to be demanded ? the

reafon

reafon is plain. It was with difficulty perfons could be had to fupply the wants of the fick, as nurfes;—applications became more and more numerous, the confequence was, when we procured them at fix dollars per week, and called upon them to go where they were wanted, found they were gone elfewhere; here was a difappointment; upon enquiring the caufe, we found, they had been allured away by others who offered greater wages, until they got from two to four dollars per day. We had no reftraint upon the people. It was natural for people in low circumftances to accept a voluntary, bounteous reward; efpecially under the loathfomnefs many of the fick, when nature fhuddered at the thought of the infection, and the tafk affigned was aggravated by lunacy, and being left much alone with them. Had Mr. Carey been folicited to fuch an undertaking, for hire, *Query*, " what would *he* have demanded ?" but Mr. Carey, although chofen a member of that band of worthies who have fo eminently diftinguifhed themfelves by their labours, for the relief of the fick and helplefs—yet, quickly after his election, left them to ftruggle with their arduous and hazardous tafk, by leaving the city. It is true Mr. Carey was no hireling, and had a right to flee, and upon his return, to plead the caufe of thofe who fled; yet, we think, he was wrong in giving fo partial and injurious an account of the black nurfes; if they have taken advantage of the public diftrefs ? Is it any more than he hath done of its defire for information. We believe he has made more money by the fale of his " fcraps" than a dozen of the greateft extortioners among the black nurfes. The great prices paid did not efcape the obfervation of that worthy and vigilant magiftrate, Matthew Clarkfon, mayor of the city, and prefident of the committee—he fent for us, and requefted we would ufe our influence, to leffen the wages of the nurfes, but on informing him the caufe, i. e. that of the people overbidding one another, it was concluded unneceffary to attempt any thing on that head; therefore it was left to the people concerned. That there were fome few black people guilty of plundering the diftreffed, we acknowledge; but in that they only are pointed out, and made mention of, we efteem partial and injurious; we know as many whites who were guilty of it; but this is looked over, while the blacks are held up to cenfure.—Is it a greater crime for a black to pilfer, than for a white to privateer ?

We

We wifh not to offend, but when an unprovoked attempt is made, to make us blacker than we are, it becomes lefs neceffary to be over cautious on that account; therefore we fhall take the liberty to tell of the conduct of fome of the whites.

We know fix pounds was demanded by, and paid to, a white woman, for putting a corpfe into a coffin; and forty dollars was demanded, and paid to four white men, for bringing it down the ftairs.

Mr. and Mrs. Taylor both died in one night; a white woman had the care of them; after they were dead fhe called on Jacob Servofs, Efq. for her pay, demanding fix pounds for laying them out; upon feeing a bundle with her, he fufpected fhe had pilfered; on fearching her, Mr. Taylor's buckles were found in her pocket, with other things.

An elderly lady, Mrs. Malony, was given into the care of a white woman, fhe died, we were called to remove the corpfe, when we came the woman was laying fo drunk that fhe did not know what we were doing, but we know fhe had one of Mrs. Malony's rings on her finger, and another in her pocket.

Mr. Carey tells us, Bufh-hill exhibited as wretched a picture of human mifery, as ever exifted. A profligate abandoned fet of nurfes and attendants (hardly any of good character could at that time be procured,) rioted on the provifions and comforts, prepared for the fick, who (unlefs at the hours when the doctors attended) were left almoft entirely deftitute of every affiftance. The dying and dead were indifcriminately mingled together. The ordure and other evacuations of the fick, were allowed to remain in the moft offenfive ftate imaginable. Not the fmalleft appearance of order or regularity exifted. It was in fact a great human flaughter-houfe, where numerous victims were immolated at the altar of intemperance.

It is unpleafant to point out the bad and unfeeling conduct of any colour, yet the defence we have undertaken obliges us to remark, that although "hardly any of good character at that time could be procured," yet only two black women were at this time in the hofpital, and they were retained and the others difcharged, when it was reduced to order and good government.

The bad confequences many of our colour apprehend from a partial relation of our conduct are, that it will prejudice the minds of the people in general againft us—becaufe it is impoffible

fible that one individual, can have knowledge of all, therefore at some future day, when some of the most virtuous, that were upon most praise-worthy motives, induced to serve the sick, may fall into the service of a family that are strangers to him, or her, and it is discovered that it is one of those stigmatised wretches, what may we suppose will be the consequence? Is it not reasonable to think the person will be abhored, despised, and perhaps dismissed from employment, to their great disadvantage, would not this be hard? and have we not therefore sufficient reason to seek for redress? We can with certainty assure the public that we have seen more humanity, more real sensibility from the poor blacks, than from the poor whites. When many of the former, of their own accord rendered services where extreme necessity called for it, the general part of the poor white people were so dismayed, that instead of attempting to be useful, they in a manner hid themselves——a remarkable instance of this——A poor afflicted dying man, stood at his chamber window, praying and beseeching every one that passed by, to help him to a drink of water; a number of white people passed, and instead of being moved by the poor man's distress, they hurried as fast as they could out of the sound of his cries—until at length a gentleman, who seemed to be a foreigner came up, he could not pass by, but had not resolution enough to go into the house, he held eight dollars in his hand, and offered it to several as a reward for giving the poor man a drink of water, but was refused by every one, until a poor black man came up, the gentleman offered the eight dollars to him, if he would relieve the poor man with a little water, " Master" replied the good natured fellow, " I will supply the gentleman with water, but surely I will not take your money for it" nor could he be prevailed upon to accept his bounty: he went in, supplied the poor object with water, and rendered him every service he could.

A poor black man, named Sampson, went constantly from house to house where distress was, and gave assistance without fee or reward; he was smote with the disorder and died, after his death his family were neglected by those he had served.

Sarah Bass, a poor black widow, gave all the assistance she could, in several families, for which she did not receive any thing; and when any thing was offered her, she left it to the option of those she served.

A 5   A woman

1ok

A woman of our colour nurfed Richard Mafon and fon, when they died, Richard's widow confidering the rifk the poor woman had run, and from obferving the fears that fometimes refted on her mind, expected fhe would have demanded fomething confiderable, but upon afking what fhe demanded, her reply was half a dollar per day. Mrs. Mafon, intimated it was not fufficient for her attendance, fhe replied it was enough for what fhe had done, and would take no more. Mrs. Mafon's feelings were fuch, that fhe fettled an annuity of fix pounds a year, on her, for life. Her name is Mary Scott.

An elderly black woman nurfed————with great diligence and attention; when recovered he afked what he muft give for her fervices——fhe replied " a dinner mafter on a cold winter's day," and thus fhe went from place to place rendering every fervice in her power without an eye to reward.

A young black woman, was requefted to attend one night upon a white man and his wife, who were very ill, no other perfon could be had;—great wages were offered her—fhe replied, I will not go for money, if I go for money God will fee it, and may be make me take the diforder and die, but if I go, and take no money, he may fpare my life. She went about nine o'clock, and found them both on the floor; fhe could procure no candle or other light, but ftaid with them about two hours, and then left them. They both died that night. She was afterward very ill with the fever—her life was fpared.

Cæfar Cranchal, a black man, offered his fervices to attend the fick, and faid, I will not take your money. I will not fell my life for money. It is faid he died with the flux.

A black lad, at the Widow Gilpin's, was intrufted with his young Mafter's keys, on his leaving the city, and tranfacted his bufinefs, with the greateft honefty, and difpatch, having unloaded a veffel for him in the time, and loaded it again.

A woman, that nurfed David Bacon, charged with exemplary moderation, and faid fhe would not have any more.

It may be faid, in vindication of the conduct of thofe, who difcovered ignorance or incapacity in nurfing, that it is, in itfelf, a confiderable art, derived from experience, as well as the exercife of the finer feelings of humanity—this experience, nine tenths of thofe employed, it is probable were wholly ftrangers to.

We

We do not recollect such acts of humanity from the poor white people, in all the round we have been engaged in. We could mention many other inftances of the like nature, but think it needlefs.

It is unpleafant for us to make thefe remarks, but juftice to our colour demands it. Mr. Carey pays William Gray and us a compliment; he fays, our fervices and others of their colour, have been very great &c. By naming us, he leaves thefe others, in the hazardous ftate of being claffed with thofe who are called the " vileft." The few that were difcovered to merit public cenfure, were brought to juftice, which ought to have fufficed, without being canvaffed over in his " Trifle" of a pamphlet—which caufes us to be more particular, and endeavour to recal the efteem of the public for our friends, and the people of colour, as far as they may be found worthy; for we conceive, and experience proves it, that an ill name is eafier given than taken away. We have many unprovoked enemies, who begrudge us the liberty we enjoy, and are glad to hear of any complaint againft our colour, be it juft or unjuft; in confequence of which we are more earneftly endeavouring all in our power, to warn, rebuke, and exhort our African friends, to keep a confcience void of offence towards God and man; and, at the fame time, would not be backward to interfere, when ftigmas or oppreffion appear pointed at, or attempted againft them, unjuftly; and, we are confident, we fhall ftand juftified in the fight of the candid and judicious for fuch conduct.

Mr. Carey's firft, fecond, and third editions, are gone forth into the world; and in all probability, have been read by thoufands that will never read his fourth—confequently, any alteration he may hereafter make, in the paragraph alluded to, cannot have the defired effect, or atone for the paft; therefore we apprehend it neceffary to publifh our thoughts on the occafion. Had Mr. Carey faid, a number of white and black wretches eagerly feized on the opportunity to extort from the diftreffed, and fome few of both were detected in plundering the fick, it might extenuate, in a great degree, the having made mention of the blacks.

We can affure the public, there were as many white as black people, detected in pilfering, although the number of the latter, employed as nurfes, was twenty times as great as the former,

and

and that there is, in our opinion, as great a proportion of white,
as of black, inclined to such practices. It is rather to be admired, that so few instances of pilfering and robbery happened,
considering the great opportunities there were for such things:
we do not know of more than five black people, suspected of
any thing clandestine, out of the great number employed; the
people were glad to get any person to assist them—a black was
preferred, because it was supposed, they were not so likely to
take the disorder, the most worthless were acceptable, so that
it would have been no cause of wonder, if twenty causes of
complaint occurred, for one that hath. It has been alledged,
that many of the sick, were neglected by the nurses; we do
not wonder at it, considering their situation, in many instances,
up night and day, without any one to relieve them, worn down
with fatigue, and want of sleep, they could not in many cases,
render that assistance, which was needful: where we visited, the
causes of complaint on this score, were not numerous. The
case of the nurses, in many instances, were deserving of commiseration, the patient raging and frightful to behold; it has frequently required two persons, to hold them from running away,
others have made attempts to jump out of a window, in many
chambers they were nailed down, and the door was kept locked,
to prevent them from running away, or breaking their necks,
others lay vomiting blood, and screaming enough to chill them
with horror. Thus were many of the nurses circumstanced,
alone, until the patient died, then called away to another scene
of distress, and thus have been for a week or ten days left to do
the best they could without any sufficient rest, many of them
having some of their dearest connections sick at the time, and
suffering for want, while their husband, wife, father, mother, &c.
have been engaged in the service of the white people. We mention this to shew the difference between this and nursing in common cases, we have suffered equally with the whites, our distress
hath been very great, but much unknown to the white people.
Few have been the whites that paid attention to us while the
black were engaged in the other's service. We can assure the
public we have taken four and five black people in a day to be
buried. In several instances when they have been seized with
the sickness while nursing, they have been turned out of the
house, and wandering and destitute until taking shelter wherever

ever they could (as many of them would not be admitted to their former homes) they have languished alone, and we know of one who even died in a stable. Others acted with more tenderness, when their nurses were taken sick they had proper care taken of them at their houses. We know of two instances of this.

It is even to this day a generally received opinion in this city, that our colour was not so liable to the sickness as the whites. We hope our friends will pardon us for setting this matter in its true state.

The public were informed that in the West-Indies and other places where this terrible malady had been, it was observed the blacks were not affected with it. Happy would it have been for you, and much more so for us, if this observation had been verified by our experience.

When the people of colour had the sickness and died, we were imposed upon, and told it was not with the prevailing sickness, until it became too notorious to be denied, then we were told some few died but not many. Thus were our services extorted *at the peril of our lives,* yet you accuse us of extorting *a little money from you.*

Tne bill of mortality for the year 1793, published by Matthew Whitehead, and John Ormrod, clerks, and Joseph Dolby, sexton, will convince any reasonable man that will examine it, that as many coloured people died in proportion as others. In 1792, there were 67 of our colour buried, and in 1793 it amounted to 305; thus the burials among us have increased more than fourfold, was not this in a great degree the effects of the services of the unjustly vilified black people?

Perhaps it may be acceptable to the reader to know how we found the sick affected by the sickness; our opportunities of hearing and seeing them have been very great. They were taken with a chill, a head-ach, a sick stomach, with pains in their limbs and back, this was the way the sickness in general began, but all were not affected alike, some appeared but slightly affected with some of these symptoms, what confirmed us in the opinion of a person being smitten was the colour of their eyes. In some it raged more furiously than others—some have languished for seven and ten days, and appeared to get better the day, or some hours before they died, while others were cut off in one, two, or three days, but their complaints were similar, Some
loft

loſt their reaſon and raged with all the fury madneſs could produce, and died in ſtrong convulſions. Others retained their
reaſon to the laſt, and ſeemed rather to fall aſleep than die. We
could not help remarking that the former were of ſtrong paſſions,
and the latter of a mild temper. Numbers died in a kind of
dejeċtion, they concluded they muſt go, (ſo the phraſe for dying was) and therefore in a kind of fixed determined ſtate of
mind went off.

It ſtruck our minds with awe, to have application made by
thoſe in health, to take charge of them in their ſickneſs, and of
their funeral. Such applications have been made to us ; many
appeared as though they thought they muſt die, and not live ;
ſome have lain on the floor, to be meaſured for their coffin and
grave. A gentleman called one evening, to requeſt a good
nurſe might be got for him, when he was ſick, and to ſuperin-
tend his funeral, and gave particular directions how he would
have it conducted, it ſeemed a ſurpriſing circumſtance, for the
man appeared at the time, to be in perfect health, but calling two
or three days after to ſee him, found a woman dead in the houſe,
and the man ſo far gone, that to adminiſter any thing for his recovery was needleſs—he died that evening. We mention this,
as an inſtance of the dejeċtion and deſpondence, that took hold
on the minds of thouſands, and are of opinion, it aggravated the
caſe of many, while others who bore up chearfully, got up
again, that probably would otherwiſe have died.

When the mortality came to its greateſt ſtage, it was impoſſi-
ble to procure ſufficient aſſiſtance, therefore many whoſe
friends, and relations had left them, died unſeen, and unaſſiſted.
We have found them in various ſituations ſome laying on the
floor, as bloody as if they had been dipt in it, without any appearance of their having had, even a drink of water for their relief ;
others laying on a bed with their cloaths on, as if they had came
in fatigued, and lain down to reſt ; ſome appeared, as if they
had fallen dead on the floor, from the poſition we found them
in.

Truly our taſk was hard, yet through mercy, we were enabled to go on.

One thing we obſerved in ſeveral inſtances—when we were
called, on the firſt appearance of the diſorder to bleed, the per-
ſon frequently, on the opening a vein before the operation was
near over, felt a change for the better, and expreſſed a relief in
their

certificate of your approbation of our conduct, fo far as it hath
come to your knowledge.

    With an affectionate regard and efteem,
       We are your friends,

                     ABSALOM JONES.

January 7th, 1794.   RICHARD ALLEN.

HAVING, during the prevalence of the late malignant diforder, had almoft daily opportunities of feeing the conduct of Abfalom Jones and Richard Allen, and the people employed by them, to bury the dead—I with cheerfulnefs give
this teftimony of my approbation of their proceedings, as far
as the fame came under my notice. Their diligence, attention
and decency of deportment, afforded me, at the time, much fatisfaction.

               MATTHEW CLARKSON, Mayor.
Philadelphia, January 23, 1794.

An Addrefs to thofe who keep Slaves, and approve the Practice.

THE judicious part of mankind will think it unreafonable,
that a fuperior good conduct is looked for, from our race,
by thofe who ftigmatize us as men, whofe bafenefs is incurable,
and may therefore be held in a ftate of fervitude, that a merciful man would not doom a beaft to; yet you try what you can
to prevent our rifing from the ftate of barbarifm, you reprefent
us to be in, but we can tell you, from a degree of experience,
that a black man, although reduced to the moft abject ftate
human nature is capable of, fhort of real madnefs, can think,
reflect, and feel injuries, although it may not be with the fame
degree of keen refentment and revenge, that you who have
been and are our great oppreffors, would manifeft, if reduced to
the pitiable condition of a flave. We believe if you would try
the experiment of taking a few black children, and cultivate
their minds with the fame care, and let them have the fame
profpect in view, as to living in the world, as you would wifh
              for

for your own children, you would find upon the trial, they were not inferior in mental endowments.

We do not wifh to make you angry, but excite your attention to confider, how hateful flavery is in the fight of that God, who hath deftroyed kings and princes, for their oppreffion of the poor flaves; Pharaoh and his princes with the pofterity of king Saul, were deftroyed by the protector and avenger of flaves. Would you not fuppofe the Ifraelites to be utterly unfit for freedom, and that it was impoffible for them to attain to any degree of excellence? Their hiftory fhews how flavery had debafed their fpirits. Men muft be wilfully blind and extremely partial, that cannot fee the contrary effects of liberty and flavery upon the mind of men; we freely confefs the vile habits often acquired in a ftate of fervitude, are not eafily thrown off; the example of the Ifraelites fhews, who with all that Mofes could do to reclaim them from it, ftill continued in their former habits more or lefs; and why will you look for better from us? Why will you look for grapes from thorns, or figs from thiftles? It is in our pofterity enjoying the fame privileges with your own, that you ought to look for better things.

When you are pleaded with, do not you reply as Pharaoh did, " wherefore do ye Mofes and Aaron, let the people from their work, behold the people of the land, now are many, and you make them reft from their burdens." We wifh you to confider, that God himfelf was the firft pleader of the caufe of flaves.

That God who knows the hearts of all men, and the propenfity of a flave to hate his oppreffor, hath ftrictly forbidden it to his chofen people, " thou fhalt not abhor an Egyptian, becaufe thou waft a ftranger in his land. Deut. xxiii. 7." The meek and humble Jefus, the great pattern of humanity, and every other virtue that can adorn and dignify men, hath commanded to love our enemies, to do good to them that hate and defpitefully ufe us. We feel the obligations, we wifh to imprefs them on the minds of our black brethren, and that we may all forgive you, as we wifh to be forgiven; we think it a great mercy to have all anger and bitternefs removed from our minds; we appeal to your own feelings, if it is not very difquieting to feel yourfelves under the dominion of a wrathful difpofition.

If you love your children, if your love your country, if you love the God of love, clear your hands from flaves, burden not your children or country with them. Our hearts have been forrowful for the late bloodfhed of the oppreffors, as well as the oppreffed, both appear guilty of each others blood, in the fight of him who faid, he that fheddeth man's blood, by man fhall his blood be fhed.

Will you, becaufe you have reduced us to the unhappy condition our colour is in, plead our incapacity for freedom, and our contented condition under oppreffion, as a fufficient caufe for keeping us under the grievous yoke! We have fhewn the caufe of our incapacity, we will alfo fhew, why we appear contented; were we to attempt to plead with our mafters, it would be deemed infolence, for which caufe they appear as contented as they can in your fight, but the dreadful infurrections they have made, when opportunity has offered, is enough to convince a reafonable man, that great uneafinefs and not contentment, is the inhabitant of their hearts.

God himfelf hath pleaded their caufe, he hath from time to time raifed up inftruments for that purpofe, fometimes mean and contemptible in your fight; at other times he hath ufed fuch as it hath pleafed him, with whom you have not thought it beneath your dignity to contend, many have been convinced of their error, condemned their former conduct, and become zealous advocates for the caufe of thofe, whom you will not fuffer to plead for themfelves.

To the People of Colour.

FEELING an engagement of mind for your welfare, we addrefs you with an affectionate fympathy, having been ourfelves flaves, and as defirous of freedom as any of you; yet the bands of bondage were fo ftrong, that no way appeared for our releafe, yet at times a hope arofe in our hearts that a way would open for it, and when our minds were mercifully vifited with the feeling of the love of God, then thefe hopes increafed, and a confidence arofe that he would make way for our enlargement,

and

and as a patient waiting was neceffary, we were very impatient, then the profpect of liberty almoft vanifhed away, and we were in darknefs and perplexity.

We mention our experience to you, that your hearts may not fink at the difcouraging profpects you may have, and that you may put your truft in God, who fees your condition, and as a merciful father pitieth his children, fo doth God pity them that love him ; and as your hearts are inclined to ferve God, you will feel an affectionate regard towards your mafters and miftreffes, and the whole family where you live, this will be feen by them, and tend to promote your liberty, efpecially with fuch as have feeling mafters, and if they are otherwife you will have the favour and love of God dwelling in your hearts, which you will value more than any thing elfe, which will be a confolation in the worft condition you can be in, and no mafter can deprive you of it ; and as life is fhort and uncertain, and the chief end of our having a being in this world, is to be prepared for a better, we wifh you to think of this more than any thing elfe : then will you have a view of that freedom which the fons of God enjoy : and if the troubles of your condition end with your lives, you will be admitted to the freedom which God hath prepared for thofe of all colours that love him ; here the power of the moft cruel matter ends and all forrow and tears are wiped away.

To you who are favoured with freedom, let your conduct manifeft your gratitude toward the compaffionate mafters who have fet you free, and let no rancour or ill-will lodge in your breafts for any bad treatment you may have received from any ; if you do, you tranfgrefs againft God, who will not hold you guiltlefs, he would not fuffer it even in his beloved people Ifrael, and can you think he will allow it unto us ?

There is much gratitude due from our colour towards the white people, very many of them are inftruments in the hand of God for our good, even fuch as have held us in captivity, are now pleading our caufe with earneftnefs and zeal ; and we are forry to fay, that too many think more of the evil, than of the good they have received, and inftead of taking the advice of their friends, turn from it with indifference ; much depends upon us for the help of our colour more than many are aware; if we are lazy and idle, the enemies of freedom plead it as a caufe why we ought not to be free, and fay we are better in a ftate of fervitude, and that giving us our liberty would be an in-

jury

jury to us, and by fuch conduct we ftrengthen the bands of oppreffion, and keep many in bondage who are more worthy than
ourfelves; we intreat you to confider the obligations we lay
under, to help forward the caufe of freedom, we who know how
bitter the cup is of which the flave hath to drink, O how ought
we to feel for thofe who yet remain in bondage? Will even
our friends excufe, will God pardon us, for the part we act in
making ftrong the hands of the enemies of our colour.

***

A fhort Addrefs to the Friends of Him who hath no Helper.

WE feel an inexpreffible gratitude towards you, who have
engaged in the caufe of the African race; you have
wrought a deliverance for many, from more than Egyptian bondage, your labours are unremitted for their complete redemption,
from the cruel fubjection they are in.   You feel our afflictions—
you fympathize with us in the heart-rending diftrefs, when the
hufband is feparated from the wife, and the parents from the
children, who are never more to meet in this world.   The tear
of fenfibility trickles from your eye, to fee the fufferings that
keep us from increafing.—Your righteous indignation is roufed
at the means taken to fupply the place of the murdered babe.
You fee our race more effectually deftroyed, than was in Pharaoh's power to effect, upon Ifrael's fons; you blow the trumpet
againft the mighty evil, you make the tyrants tremble; you
ftrive to raife the flave, to the dignity of a man; you take our
children by the hand, to lead them in the path of virtue, by
your care of their education; you are not afhamed to call the
moft abject of our race, brethren, children of one father, who
made of one blood all the nations of the earth. You afk for this,
nothing for yourfelves, nothing but what is worthy the caufe you
are engaged in; nothing but that we would be friends to ourfelves, and not ftrengthen the bands of oppreffion, by an evil conduct, when led out of the houfe of bondage.   May he, who hath
arifen to plead our caufe, and engaged you as volunteers in the
fervice, add to your numbers until the princes fhall come forth
from Egypt, and Ethiopia ftretch out her hand unto God.

ABSALOM JONES,
RICHARD ALLEN.

YE Minifters, that are call'd to preaching
    Teachers, and exhorters too ;
Awake! behold your harveft wafting !
    Arife! there is no reft for you.

To think upon that ftrict commandment,
    That God has on his teachers laid,
The finner's blood, who dies unwarned,
    Shall fall upon their Shepherd's head.

But oh! dear brethren, let's be doing,
    Behold the nation's in diftrefs,
The Lord of Hofts forbid their ruin,
    Before the day of grace is paft.

We read of wars and great commotions,
    Before the great and dreadful day,
Oh! Sinners, turn your finful courfes,
    And trifle not your time away.

But, oh! dear finners, that's not all that's dreadful !
    You muft before your God appear !
To give an account of your tranfactions,
    And how you fpent your time, when here.

F I N I S.

———

DANIEL COKER

*A Dialogue Between a Virginian
and an African Minister*

:

A

DIALOGUE

BETWEEN A

VIRGINIAN AND AN AFRICAN MINISTER,

WRITTEN BY THE

REV. DANIEL COKER,
A descendant of Africa....Minister of the African Methodist
Episcopal Church in Baltimore.

HUMBLY DEDICATED

TO THE

People of Colour in the United States of America.

BALTIMORE :
PRINTED BY BENJAMIN EDES,
FOR JOSEPH JAMES.
....
1810.

DIALOGUE.

" *I said, I will answer also my part ; I also will show mine opinion, for I am full of matter ; the spirit within me constraineth me.* JOB. xxxii. 17, 18.

(Therefore) " *Suffer me that I may speak ; and after that I have spoken, mock on.* JOB, xxi. 3.

Virginian. GOOD morning sir. As I had some business in town this morning, I thought that I would call on you for the purpose of holding a little conversation.

Minister. Sir, I am happy to see you ; pray take a seat.

Virginian. Sir, I have heard of you in the place of my residence, and having understood that you have had a greater opportunity of acquiring information, than those of your colour generally have ; and being informed at the

4

same time, that you were a person professing the Christian religion; I thought it would afford me some degree of satisfaction to have an interview with you.

Minister. Sir, I can assure you, that I feel my heart to glow with gratitude to that God, who has his ways in the whirlwind, and his paths through the great deep; and whose footsteps are not known; for putting it into your mind, to condescend so low, as to visit one of the descendants of the African race. And since you have done me this great honour, it will be with infinite pleasure that I shall banish every other concern in order to spend a few hours in your company.

Virginian. Sir, your civility gives me much pleasure, and I am already convinced of the good that results from religion, and literary improvements; and I flatter myself that my visit will be somewhat advantageous to me. But (that I may no longer keep you in suspense) I will hasten to inform you that I have been told you have imbibed a strange opinion, which, I think is repugnant to reason and justice.

Minister. Sir, I perceive by your conversation, that there is something on your mind,

of importance, and in order that no advantage
be taken of me, for conversing freely with you
on the subject, whatever it may be, there is a
gentleman in the next room whom I will call, if
you have no objection, and we will make a re-
capitulation of what has passed in conversation,
so that he may pen it down.

Virginian. Yes sir, by all means.

Minister. Mr. C. will you be so good as
to walk into this room?

(Mr. C. being seated, and having received
pen, ink, and paper, began to write.)

Virginian. Sir, I have understood that you
have advanced an opinion that it would be just
in our legislature to enact a law, for the emancipation of our slaves that we hold as our property; and I think I can convince you, that it
would be wrong in the highest degree.

Minister. Sir, I will hear you with pleasure.

Virginian. You will observe sir, in the first
place, that negroes were made slaves by law;
they were converted into property by an act of
the legislature, and under the sanction of that
law, I purchased them; they therefore become
my property, and I have a legal right to them
To repeal that law in order to annihilate slave-

ry, would be, violently to destroy, what I legally purchased with my money or inherited
from my father. It would be equally unjust
with dispossessing me of my horses, cattle or
any other species of property. To dispossess
me of their children, would be equally unjust
with dispossessing me of the annual profits of
my estate.

Minister. That is an important objection,
and it calls for a serious answer. The matter
seems to stand thus. Many years ago, men
being deprived of their natural rights to freedom, and made slaves, were by law converted
into property. This law, it is true, was wrong;
it established iniquity; it was against the law
of humanity, common sense, reason and conscience. It was, however, a law, and under the
sanction of it, a number of men, regardless of
its iniquity, purchased these slaves, and made
their fellow men their property. But the question is concerning the liberty of a man. The
man himself claims it as his own property. He
pleads, (and I think in truth) that it was originally his own; that he has never forfeited, nor
alienated it; and therefore, by the common
laws of justice and humanity, it is still his own.
The purchaser of the slave claims the same

property. He pleads that he purchased it under the sanction of a law, enacted by the legislature, and therefore it became his. Now, the question is, who has the best claim? Did the property in question belong to the legislature? Was it vested in them? I answer, no; it was not in them collectively, and therefore they could not convey it to those they represent. Now, does the property belong to him, who claims it from the legislature that had it not to give, or to the original owner who has never forfeited, nor alienated his right? For instance; should a law pass to sell a man's head, and should I purchase it, have I, in consequence of this law and this purchase, a better claim to this man's head than himself? Therefore, freeing men, in my opinion, is not depriving any one of their property, but restoring it to the right owner; it is suffering the unlawful captive to escape. " *Turn again our captivity O Lord, as the streams in the south.*" PSAL. cxxvi. 4. It is not wronging the master, but doing justice to the slave, restoring him to himself. The master, it is true, is wronged, he may suffer, and that greatly; but this is his own fault, and the fault of the enslaving law, and not of the law that does justice to the oppressed. You say, a law

of emancipation would be unjust, because it
would deprive men of their property; but is
there no injustice on the other side? Let us
consider the injustice on both sides, and weigh
them in an even balance. On one hand, we see
a man deprived of all property; of all capacity
to possess property; of his own free agency;
of the means of instruction; of his wife and
children; and, of almost every thing dear to
him: on the other, a man deprived of eighty
or one hundred pounds. Shall we hesitate a
moment to determine who is the greatest suf-
ferer, and who is treated with the greatest injustice? The matter appears quite glaring, when
we consider that " *neither this man nor his parents had sinned.*" JOHN, ix. 3. that he was
born to these sufferings; but the other suffers
altogether for his own sin, and that of his parents or predecessors.

Virginian. You astonish me! and I am
ready to say with one of old " *Thou hast hid
these things from the wise and prudent, and hast
revealed them unto babes.*" MATT. xi. 29. But,
sir, I have another objection, and that is this.
You say that the legislature made them slaves.
I say not so, for the Africans enslave one another, and we only purchased those who they

made prisoners of war, and reduced to slavery. Pray what will you say to this objection.

Minister. Making prisoners of war slaves, though practised by the Romans and other ancient nations, and though still practised by some barbarous tribes, can, by no means, be justified; it is unreasonable and cruel. Whatever may be said of the chief authors and promoters of an unjust war, the common soldier, who is under command and obliged to obey, and (as is often the case) deprived of the means of information as to the ground of the war, certainly cannot be thought guilty of a crime so heinous, that for it, himself and posterity, deserve the dreadful punishment of perpetual servitude. It is a cruelty that the present practice of all civilized nations, bears testimony against. Allow the objection to be true; yet, it will not justify you in the practice of enslaving the Africans; but the matter contained in your objection, is only true in part. The history of the slave trade is too tragical to be read without a bleeding heart, and weeping eyes. A few of these unhappy Africans, comparatively very few, are criminals, whose servitude is inflicted as a punishment for their crimes. The main body are innocent, unsuspecting creatures, free,

living in peace, doing nothing to forfeit the
common privileges of men; they are taken or
violently borne away, by armed force, from
their tender connections; treated with an in-
dignity, and indecency shameful to mention;
and a cruelty, shocking to all the tender feelings of humanity, and they and their posterity,
forced into a state of servitude and wretchedness for ever. It is true they are commonly
taken prisoners by Africans; but it is the en-
couragement given by Europeans that tempts
them to carry on the unprovoked wars. They
furnish them with the means, and hold out to
them a reward for their plunder. If the Africans
are thieves, the Europeans stand ready to receive
the stolen goods; if the former are robbers, the
latter furnish them with arms, and purchase
the spoil. In this case, who is the most criminal, the civilized European or the untutored
African? The European merchants know, that
they themselves are the great encouragers of
these wars, as they are the principal gainers by
the event; they know that they purchase these
slaves of those, who have no just pretence to
claim them as theirs. The African can give
the European no better claim than he himself
has; the European can give a second purchas-

er no better claim than is vested in him; and that is, a claim founded only on violence or fraud. In confirmation of this account, might be produced many substantial vouchers, and some who have spent much of their time in this nefarious traffick : but such as are accustomed to listen to the melancholy tales of this unfortunate race, cannot want sufficient evidence : those who have seen multitudes of poor innocent children driven to market and sold like beasts, have it demonstrated before their eyes.

Virginian. Stop sir, you have said enough ; I am convinced by the cogency of your argument, that we are more in fault (as you have justly observed) than the uncivilized Africans. But why do we spend time in talking about the injustice of the slave trade, when we know that it is, by an act of congress abolished.

Minister. Yes sir, and it is with gratitude I speak it, yea, to the great honour of Mr. Jefferson, late president of these United States, and also the congress that passed it, who shall ever be remembered in my prayers, for the blessing of God on them, and their families ; and I hope that a grateful remembrance of their humanity in passing that law, will engrave their names on every heart that is warmed with the least drop of African blood, to latest posterity.

Virginian. I am glad to find that you are not tainted with ingratitude.

Minister. But there is a species of the slave trade still carried on in some parts of the United States, which is equally cruel. A class of men, whose minds seem to have become almost callous to every tender feeling; who (having agents in various places, suited to their purpose) travel through different states, and by purchase or otherwise, procure a considerable number of this people; which consequently occasions a separation of the nearest relations in life. Husbands from wives, and parents from children; they are taken in droves, through the country, like herds of cattle, but with less commiseration; for being chained or otherwise fettered, the weight and friction of their shackles, naturally produces much soreness and pain. Sir, I perceive you weep (and well you may) but in addition to this, they are greatly incommoded in their travel. Jails, designed for the security of such as have forfeited their liberty by a breach of the laws, are made receptacles for this kind of merchandise; and when opportunity presents for moving them further, it is generally performed in the dead of the night, that their cries might not be heard, nor legal means used to restore the rights of such as have been kidnapped. Others are chained in the garrets or cellars of private houses, until the number becoming nearly equal to the success which might have been expected, they are then conveyed on board, and crouded under the hatches of vessels secretly stationed for that purpose, and thus transported to Petersburg in Virginia or such other parts that will ensure the best market; and many others are marched by land to unknown destined places. " Is it not" says Mr. John Parrish " a melancholy circumstance that such an abominable trade should be suffered in a land boasting of liberty?" for, says the same author "while I was waiting, with other friends, on the legislature of Maryland, at their session in 1803, it was well known, that a vessel lay in the river, below Baltimore, to take in slaves; a practice common on the waters of Maryland, Delaware, and some other places. On our presentation" says he "of friends memorial, a committee being appointed, reported : one, that it was reasonable, an act should pass to prevent husbands being separated from wives, and parents from children, under ten years of age; the other, to prevent persons set free, at a given time, by will or otherwise, from being sold and carried out of the state; but neither of these objects could be obtained." The flagrant violation of the rights of humanity was set forth in an humble manner, by the Rev. Absalom Jones, and Mr. James Forten of Philadelphia, in their petition to congress at one of their sessions, held in Philadelphia, in behalf of their suffering brethren in captivity; but were their petitions granted? No. But as I believe you feel the force of my argument, and consent to the awful truths, I will stop to hear, if you have any other objection to offer against a law of emancipation.

Virginian. Sir, I must confess that there is such a trade existing in the United States, and must also acknowledge that it is a cruel one; but still, I have objections to a law of emancipation.

Minister. Pray sir, what are your objections? Bring them forward, and I will try to answer them.

Virginian. I said I had objections to offer against a law of emancipation, but that is not all; I have something to offer in favour of slavery.

Minister. Sir, I am astonished to hear you say, that you have something to offer in favour of slavery.

Virginian. You are astonished, ah, but I think you will be more surprised when I tell you that I shall draw my argument from the scriptures, and I suppose you will not call them in question, or rail against what they tolerate. Pray have you ever studied divinity?

Minister. No sir, I have never studied it in the way which I expect you mean, that is, so as (by the common method of a collegiate education) to be titled Rev. D. C——, D. D. but, let this be as it may, God can teach me by his spirit to understand his word. Pray let me hear, or rather let me see the scripture that tolerates this worst of evils.

Virginian. By all means. Have you a bible?

Minister. Yes sir, I should be sorry if I had not, for I live on " *the sincere milk of the word.*" 1 PET. ii. 2. Here is the bible sir.

Virginian. Well sir, will you please to find it? for I seldom read the bible; but I think I have heard our minister quote a passage of scripture to prove that slavery was just. But I know the ministers of your denomination will not allow that slavery is consistent with justice; indeed I am told that your bishop preaches against it, and for that reason I dont like him, nor indeed any of the methodist society; for they have made a law in their discipline against it, and to tell the truth, I think they are almost as bad as the quakers, only they do not send so many memorials to the different legislatures in behalf of the freedom of the negroes; but they are forever preaching against slavery (as I understand) and have been instrumental in bringing about the freedom of some thousands in the United States. However, all clergymen dont think as they do.

Minister. Sir, as to that, I have but little to say, and that is, they will, no doubt, have their influence. But you wished I would find the text that supported slavery; and how I shall do that I cannot tell, unless I should add a little; and you know, that is strictly forbidden; (REV. xxii. 18.) for I dont think that there is any scripture to support it. Can you think of any part of it? for I have a very excellent Concordance which I think will enable you to find it, if it is within the lids of the bible.

Virginian. I think it is something about Abraham's having slaves. I wish you would look, for I dont know what you mean by a concordance.

Minister. Well sir, I expect I know what you refer to. If I read it, will you know whether it is the same you mean?

Virginian. Yes sir.

Minister. Well sir, the scripture to which I think you refer, reads thus, " *He that is born in thy house, and he that is bought with thy money, must needs be circumcised.*" &c. GEN. xvii. 13. Now, I suppose your minister undertook to infer from this, that as Abraham had slaves, and as he bought them with money, therefore to make slaves of the Africans must be right.

Virginian. Yes sir. That is the scripture, and that was the inference (and I think a just one,) but that was not the only text that he quoted.

Minister. Pray sir, what is the other?

Virginian. Why sir, it is, where Paul says, " *Servants obey your masters*" or words to that effect.

Minister. You have not quoted the text right, sir. Here is the bible; read COL. iii. 22.

Virginian. I see my mistake. It reads " *Servants obey in all things your masters.*

Minister. Well; we will attend to the first text referred to, concerning Abraham's having bought servants in his house.

Virginian. Stop sir. Let me tell you what our minister inferred from it. From the passage in Genesis, he argued, that since **Abraham** had servants born in his house, and bought with money, they must have served for life, like our negroes ; and hence he concluded that it was lawful for us to purchase heathens for servants ; and if they had children born in our houses, to make them servants also. From the law of Moses, he argued that the Israelites were authorized to leave the children of their servants, as an inheritance to their own children forever ; he said also, that if this was immoral in itself, a just God would never have given it the sanction of his authority ; and if lawful in itself, said he, we may safely follow the example of faithful Abraham, or act according to the law of Moses.

Minister. You will grant the scriptures to be of Divine authority ; you will also grant, that they are consistent with themselves, and that one passage may help to explain another : grant me this, and then I reply to your argument in favour of slavery.

Virginian. By all means.

Minister. In the thirteenth verse of the seventeenth chapter of Genesis, we find that Abraham was commanded to circumcise all

that were born in his house or bought with
money : we find in the sequel of the chapter,
that he obeyed the command without delay,
and actually circumcised every male in his family who came under this description. This law
of circumcision continued in force, it was not
abrogated, but confirmed by the law of Moses.
Now, to the circumcised, were committed the
oracles of God; and circumcision was a token
of that covenant, by which (among other
things) the land of Canaan, and the various privileges in it, were promised to Abraham and
his seed, and to all that were included in that
covenant. All were included, to whom circumcision (which was the token of the covenant) was administered, agreeably to God's
command. By Divine appointment, not only
Abraham, and his natural seed, but he that was
bought with money, of any stranger that was
not of his seed, was circumcised. Since the
seed of the stranger received the token of this
covenant, we must believe that he was included
and interested in 'it ; that the benefits promised,
were to be conferred on him. These persons
bought with money, were no longer looked
upon as uncircumcised and unclean; as aliens
and strangers; but were incorporated with the

church and nation of the Israelites, and became
one people with them; became God's covenant
people. Whence it appears, that suitable provision was made by the divine law, that they
should be properly educated, made free, and
enjoy all the common privileges of citizens. It
was, by the divine law enjoined upon the Israelites, thus to circumcise all the males born in
their houses; then, if the purchased servants in
question, had any children, their masters were
bound by law to incorporate them into their
church and nation. The children then were
the servants of the Lord, in the same sense
as the natural descendants of Abraham were;
and therefore, according to the law, LEV. xxv.
42, 54. they could not be made slaves. *"For
they are my servants, which I brought forth out
of the land of Egypt : they shall not be sold as
bondmen. And if he be not redeemed in these
years, then he shall go out in the year of Jubilee, both he, and his children with him."* The
passage of scripture under consideration was so
far from authorizing the Israelites to make
slaves of their servants children, that they evidently forbid it ; and therefore, are so far from
proving the lawfulness of your enslaving the
children of the Africans, that they clearly con-

demn the practice as criminal. These passages of sacred writ have been wickedly pressed into the service of mammon perhaps more frequently than any others. But does it not now appear, that these weighty pieces of artillery may be fairly wrested from your minister, and turned upon the hosts of the mammonites, with very good effect? The minister you speak of, who plead for slavery from this passage of scripture, should have observed, that in the law of Moses referred to, there is not the least mention made of the children of these servants; it is not said they should be servants or any thing about them. No doubt some of them had children; but it was unnecessary to mention them, because they were already provided for, by the law of circumcision. To extend the law of Moses to the children of these servants, is arbitrary and presumptuous; it is making them to include much more than is expressed or necessarily implied in the text. And, it is not binding on me to prove how these persons were made servants at first; nor is it necessary we should know whether they were persons who had forfeited their liberty by capital crimes; or whether they had involved themselves in debt by folly or extravagance, and submitted to serve during their lives, in order to avoid a greater calamity; or whether they were driven to that necessity in their younger days, for want of friends to take care of them. We are not informed, whatever may be conjectured. This, however, we may be certain of, that the Israelites were not sent by a divine mandate, to nations three hundred miles distant, who were neither doing, nor meditating any thing against them, and to whom they had no right whatever, in order to captivate them by fraud or force; tare them away from their native country, and all their tender connections; bind them in chains and fetters; croud them into ships, and there murder them by thousands, for want of air and proper exercise; and then doom the survivors and their posterity to bondage and misery forever.

Virginian. Hold sir, you have said sufficient. I am sorry I mentioned the text: but I had no idea of your being able to give such an explanation of it. Pray sir, where did you study divinity?

Minister. In the school of Christ. And that is the best place for a gospel minister to take his degrees. But sir, I think you said something about saint Paul.

Virginian. Yes sir. But I am quite easy about bringing it forward; for you explain scripture so different from our minister, that I am afraid it will be of but little use to me, that is, in favour of holding the Africans in unconditional bondage. However, the text that I alluded to, is, where saint Paul says, *" Servants obey in all things your masters.*

Minister. Sir, in order, rightly to understand the matter, we should recollect the situation of Christians at that time. They were under the Roman yoke; the government at that time was in the hands of the heathens who were watching for every opportunity to charge them with designs against it, in order to justify their bloody persecution. But ours is not a heathen, but is called a Christian government, so that the Christians are not, by it, persecuted unto death. In such circumstances, therefore, had the apostle proclaimed liberty to the slaves, it would probably have exposed many of them to certain destruction, and injured the cause he loved so well, and that without the prospect of freeing one single individual; which would have been the height of madness and cruelty. Therefore it was wisdom in him, not to say a single word about freedom, more than he did.

Virginian. More than he did, you say! But did he say any thing about it yea or nay?

Minister. Yes sir, he said " *If thou mayest be made free, use it rather.*"

Virginian. Shew me that sir.

Minister. Here it is; 1 COR. vii. 21.

Virginian. I see it is so, and I wonder that our minister never quoted this text in favour of freedom! It appears, that like Ananias and Saphira, ACTS v. 5,—10, he kept some part back. But I hope God will not make such an example of him.

Minister. I hope not, sir. You say that you wonder, but you need not, for it is likely your minister thought, that if you should free your slaves, you could not afford to pay him so large a salary.

Virginian. Well, perhaps that was it. But, although what you have said appears to be the height of reason, yet I have several objections more to make.

Minister. Stop sir, if you please, and let me finish.

Virginian. By all means; I thought you was done.

Minister. No sir; for I would observe, that though the apostle acted with this prudent

reserve, the unreasonableness of perpetual unconditional slavery, may be easily inferred from
the righteous and benevolent doctrines and duties, taught in the New Testament. It is very
evident, that slavery is contrary to the spirit
and nature of the Christian religion. It is contrary to that most excellent precept, laid down
by the Divine Author of the Christian establishment, viz. "*Whatsoever ye would that men
should do to you, do ye even so to them; for
this is the law and the prophets.*" MATT. vii. 12.

Virginian. That is a hard saying, although
I know it is a divine precept.

Minister. Hard as it may appear, yet it is
a precept that is finely calculated to teach the
duties of justice; to enforce their obligations,
and persuade the mind to obedience, so that
nothing can excel it. No man, when he views
the hardships and misery, the boundless labours, the unreasonable punishments, the separation between loving husbands and wives, between affectionate parents and children, can
say, in truth, were I in their place, I should
be contented; that would say, I so far approve
of such usage, as to believe, the law that subjects me to it, is perfectly right; that I and my
offspring should be denied the protection of

c

law, and yet by the same law to be bound to
suffer all these calamities, though I never forfeited my freedom, nor merited such cruel
treatment more than others.—No sir. There is
a vicegerent in our breast that bears testimony
against this, as unreason able and wicked. "*He
hath shewed thee, O man, what is good; and
what doth the Lord require of thee, but to do
justly, and love mercy, and to walk humbly with
thy God.*" MICAH vi. 8.

Virginian. Sir, you have said sufficient. I
am convinced that slavery is a great evil; but
I think that greater evils would arise from a
law of emancipation.

Minister. Sir, I am surprised! but my astonishment is not argument, therefore, let me
hear those evils that you think would result
from a law of emancipation, that I may answer
them.

Virginian. Well sir; in the first place,
slaves are unacquainted with the arts of life,
being used to act only under the direction of
others; they have never acquired the habits of
industry; have not that sense of propriety, and
spirit of emulation, necessary to make them
useful members of civil society. Many have
been so accustomed to the meaner vices; habit-

uated to lying, pilfering, and stealing, so that
when pinched with want, they would commit
these crimes, become pests to society, or end
their days on the gallows. Here are evils on
both sides, and of two evils we should take the
least.

Minister. Sir, I agree that when there are
two natural evils before us, we should choose
the least; but when two moral evils are before
us we should choose neither. To hold men in
perpetual bondage is a moral evil. And here
I must do as David did, SAM. xvii. 51. that is,
take your weapon to destroy this mighty Goli-
ath, For you have very justly observed, that
holding these men in slavery is the cause of
their plunging into such vicious habits as lying,
pilfering, and stealing; then I say, remove the
cause, that the effects may cease. That for
free men, whether white or black, to steal, lie
or pilfer, is evidently a dreadful thing, and for
this reason, the path which necessarily leads so
directly to it, should the more speedily be ob-
structed. For, " *A prudent man foreseeth the
evil, and hideth himself: but the simple pass on,
and are punished.*" PROV. xxii. 3. But are
these evils confined to a people of a sable countenance? No sir, experience tells us otherwise.

Therefore to reason consistently, you should
say, that every man, whether white or black,
that lies, steals or pilfers, should be made
slaves. Now sir, what say you to this?

Virginian. I am sorry I mentioned what I
did, for I confess that it is an argument more
against slavery than for it: but I have still another objection to offer against a law of emancipation.

Minister. What is your other objection?
for I think you are beginning to glean.

Virginian. Should we set our slaves free,
it would lay a foundation for intermarriages,
and an unnatural mixture of blood, and our
posterity at length would all be mulattoes.

Minister. This, I confess, would be a very
alarming circumstance, but I think your conclusion is entirely wrong; for it is a rare thing
indeed, to see black men with white wives;
and when such instances occur, those men are
generally of the lowest class, and are despised
by their own people. For Divine Providence
(as if in order to perpetuate the distinction of
colour) has not only placed those different nations at a great distance from each other; but
a natural aversion and disgust seems to be im-
planted in the breast of each. For captain

Philip Beavor, in his African memoranda, relates, that "one of the white women of the
company of adventurers to the island of Bula-
ma, being taken captive by the natives, no violation of her chastity was offered, owing probably, to the extreme antipathy they have to a
white skin, which they fully evidence on several
occasions." But sir, is it not surprising, that
some of high rank, and who profess abhorrence
to such connections, have been first in the
transgression? But suppose it should be the
cause of intermarriages, (which I am far from
believing,) and the number of mulattoes aug-
mented, you should recollect that it is too late
to prevent this evil; the matter is already gone
beyond recovery; for it may be proved with
mathematical certainty, that if things go on in
the present course, the future inhabitants of
America will be much checkered. For instance, visit some of the gentleman's seats that
abound with slaves, and see how children of
different complexions, swarm on every side:
for all the children of mulattoes, will be mulattoes, and the whites are daily enhancing the
number; which you know is an undeniable
truth. Thus this realized evil is coming about
in a way, truly disgraceful to both colours.

c 2

Fathers will have their own children for slaves;
men will possess their own brothers and sisters
for property, and leave them to their heirs, or
sell them to strangers for life; and youths will
have their old grey headed uncles and aunts,
for slaves. This is not imagination or falsehood : it has been, and (I fear) is still the case.
O that this, sir, which calls aloud for ven-
geance, were exterminated from the face of the
earth. For, hear what the Lord saith by the
mouth of his prophet, " *Ah sinful nation, a people laden with iniquity, a seed of evil doers,
children that are corrupters! They have for-
saken the Lord, they have provoked the Holy
One of Israel unto anger, they are gone away
backward.*" ISAIAH i. 4.

Virginian. Sir, I have not another objection
to offer, but at the same time, I am of the opinion, that if I was to make my slaves an offer
of their liberty, they would not accept of it.

Minister. I know that I have heard some
of my colour talk in this strange way, but I
know of no better way for you to clear your
skirts of their blood, than to take the scripture
for your guide

Virginian. Why sir, does the scripture say
any thing on this subject?

Minister. Yes sir. And I think, something much to the purpose.

Virginian. Pray sir, show me it, or let me hear it.

Minister. My son, hand father the bible.— Well sir, it reads thus ; " *And if the servant shall plainly say, I love my master, my wife and my children ; I will not go out free : then his master shall bring him unto the judges ; he shall also bring him to the door, or unto the door post : and his master shall bore his ear through with an awl ; and he shall serve him forever.*" EXODUS xxi. 5, 6.

Virginian. Well sir, I have fifty-five negroes ; and I will return home, and make them all (that are of age) an offer of their freedom ; and those that will not go, according to that passage you have now read, I shall be justified in keeping as slaves.

Minister. Yes sir. But let me tell you how you ought (in my opinion) to use those that will not go (though I don't think there will be many) that is, to treat them well, and consider them as men providentially placed under your care; and show yourself a faithful guardian, by giving them a Christian education, and providing them a sufficiency of the necessaries of life;

and do not (for God's sake) follow the example
of many slave holders in Virginia, who, allow
their slaves but one peck of meal for a whole
week.   How despotically are they ruled!
instead of receiving kind and gentle treatment,
they are subjected to cruelty and oppression;
by masters, mistreses, and hard hearted
overseers.   It is shocking to the feelings of
humanity, in travelling through some parts of
the state of Virginia, to see the poor objects
(especially in the inclement season) in rags,
and many of the females in a manner naked,
and trembling with the cold.   And yet some
of these masters will have the face to say, they
treat their slaves well.   Custom may have
reconciled it to them, but it strikes the feeling
minds of strangers with horror and sympathy.

A chief of the Seneca Indians, who had
been at the seat of government and beheld
the oppression these people laboured under,
afterwards inquired whether the quakers kept
slaves; on being informed they did not he expressed great satisfaction: mentioned he had
been at the City of Washington, and found
many white people kept blacks in slavery,
and used them no better than horses.   That
pious man Richard Baxter, treating on the

subject, says, that " it is enough to make the
heathen hate Christianity," which was verified
by a late well authenticated fact: several mis-
sionaries being sent out professedly to propa-
gate the gospel among the aborigines of the wil-
derness, on informing them of their mission, the
Indians held a council for upwards of ten days;
and at length advised them to return home—
that the white people made slaves of the black
people, and if they had it in their power, they
would make slaves of the Indians; they therefore wanted no such religion. If professors of
Christianity would pay more attention to the
exhortation of the apostle, "*Giving no offence
in any thing, that the ministry be not blamed.*"
2 COR. vi. 3. then would the prejudice of the
heathens to the Christian religion, fall to rise no
more. Another dreadful consequence of slavery, is this, although the slave is a moral agent,
and an accountable creature, and is a capable subject of religion and morality; yet many
of them, are by their wicked master (so called)
deprived of instruction in the doctrine, and
duties of religion; and some masters have actually had recourse to the lash, to effect the same.
Some, I said, for thank God, all masters are
not so abominably wicked; for, I remember

hearing dear old Bishop Asbury the last time
he preached in the African church in the city
of Baltimore, say, that in some parts of the
southern states, there are some owners of slaves
who take pleasure in seeing their servants get
religion. And is it not too obvious, that those
masters who try to keep their slaves from the
means of instruction, do it in order to keep
them in a state of ignorance, lest they should
become too wise to answer their selfish purposes and too knowing to rest easy, and satisfied
in their degraded situation? and now sir, if you
will have a little patience I will give you a
relation of the experience of one of those suffer-
ers, that I have been speaking of and I will
give it in his own words. " First," says he
" I am chained, and kept back from my public
meetings; secondly, I am chained in and out
of the house for thirty and some times forty
hours together, without the least nourishment,
under the sun; thirdly, I am tied and stretched
on the ground, as my blessed master was, and
suffer the owner of my body to cut my flesh,
until pounds of blood, which came from my
body, would congeal and cling to the soals of
my shoes, and pave my way for several yards.
When he would have satisfied his thirst in spil-

ling my blood, he would turn from me to refresh himself with his bottle."

Virginian. Stop sir. Let that be concealed from a christian nation.

Minister. No sir, I cannot stop, for I have not done with my suffering brother's experience: but I will read you a passage of scripture that strikes my mind. "*For behold, the Lord cometh out of his place, to punish the inhabitants of the earth for their iniquity: the earth also shall disclose her blood, and shall no more cover her slain.*" ISAIAH xxvi. 21.

Virginian. Well sir, go on to finish the experience of this negro, since I find from that scripture, it will ere long, be known.

Minister. Well, and said my poor brother, " He would then leave me to renounce my religion, and the God that made me. But all in vain. When l looked and saw my blood running so free, my heart could not help praising my Saviour, and thanking God that he had given me the privilege, and endowed me with fortitude sufficient to bear it without murmuring. My master finding this a great means to make me more fervent in prayer, bethought himself of another diabolical stratagem to put me to shame, which he put into execution, viz.

carried me like a malefactor to a neighbouring
blacksmith, and there had an iron collar rivet-
ed around my neck as though I was a deserter
or was about to make an elopement; and then
with kicks and cuffs, I was led away and clapt
in a field to labour, although scarce able : but
thank God Almighty, when I recollected that
my dear Lord and Master had commanded me
to bear my cross, and take his yoke upon me,
my soul, my heart, was elevated. I thought I
could have flown, and I went to work with
more submission, and with more apparent love
than I had done heretofore."

Virginian. Sir, I give you my word, that,
if any should think proper to stay with me, I
will use them as well as my own children.

Minister. Well, thank God for such a determination. But there is one thing more that
I would request of you, and that is, before you
die, make it in your will, that at your death,
those slaves who may wish to continue with you
shall be free; for your children, or heirs, A,
B, or C, may not be of your humane disposition, for very profligate, and cruel children
sometimes spring from very pious and benevolent parents.

Virginian. I am glad you mentioned that, for I might not have thought of it. And now let me remind you of what I first said, that is, perhaps my interviews with you would not be in vain, and so I have found it, and I do assure you, if I had my will, there should not be a slave in the United States. But how this could be brought about, I cannot see. Pray let me hear your ideas on this matter.

Minister. Sir, that is an important question, and has been asked more than once, and therefore, I think it will be best for me to read you a piece out of Mr. Parrish's remarks, which I think is much to the purpose.

Virginian. Sir, I should like to hear it

Minister. Well sir, it reads as follows. " It has been frequently asked, ' How can the United States get rid of slavery ?' This is an Important question. The immediate liberation of all the slaves, may be attended with some difficulty; but surely something towards it, now may be done. In the first place, let the president's plan, (inserted in his notes on Virginia,) be adopted, fixing a period, after which none should be born slaves in the United States; and the coloured children to be free at a certain age. This would tend to quiet the

D

minds of the aged, affording the consoling prospect that their offspring, in a future day will
enjoy the blessings of liberty : and let no legal
barrier remain to prevent individuals freeing
their slaves at pleasure ; and thus, in due time,
a gradual emancipation would take place, and
be fully completed. The Spanish mode for the
gradual abolition of slavery, is praise-worthy.
They are registered in a book provided for that
purpose, and one day in each week allowed
them as their own : when they have earned a
stipulated sum, another day in the week is
added ; thus going on, they have an opportunity of acquiring as much as will purchase their
entire freedom ; which, at the same time that
it accomplishes the desired end, inures them to
habits of industry, and prompts to commenda-
ble economy.

Virginian. Sir, I am satisfied that *that*
might, and in my opinion, ought to be done.

Minister. Well sir, I am happy that I have
made a proselyte of you, to humanity, and not
such a one as is delineated in MATT. xxiii. 15.

Virginian. Well my dear friend, I should
be happy to spend more time with you, about
the salvation of my poor soul, but I hope to
see you again before it be long. Farewell.

Minister. And the Lord be with you.

Mr. C. Well sir, I am highly gratified with the conversation that I have witnessed, although I have not been able to pay that attention that I could have wished, in consequence of my having to make a memorandum of the same.

Minister. Well sir, for our satisfaction, please to read it over.

Mr. C. With pleasure sir. It reads as follows.——I think you had better have it published.

Minister. I think I will, although I am persuaded at the same time, that in so doing I shall expose my own imbecility.

·············

The following will show what God is doing for Ethiopia's sons in the United States of America.

" But ye are a chosen generation, a royal priesthood, and an holy nation, a peculiar people ; that ye should shew forth the praise of him who hath called you out of darkness into his marvellous light: which in time past were not a people, but are now the people of God : which had not obtained

mercy, but now have obtained mercy." 1 PETER, ii. **9, 10.**

A LIST

OF THE NAMES OF THE AFRICAN MINISTERS WHO ARE IN HOLY ORDERS, OF THE AUTHOR'S ACQUAINTANCE.

Rev. Richard Allen, Pastor of the African Methodist Episcopal church.—*Philadelphia.*

Rev. Absalom Jones, Rector of St. Thomas's, a Protestant church.—*Philadelphia.*

Rev. Mr. Tapsicho,	Methodist,	*Philadelphia.*
Rev. James Champin,	do.	**do.**
Rev. Jeffrey Buley,	do.	**do.**
Rev. Abraham Thompson,	do.	*New York.*
Rev. James Varrick,	do.	**do.**
Rev. William Miller,	do.	**do.**
Rev. June Scott	do.	**do.**
Rev. Benjamin Paul	Baptist	**do.**
Rev. Mr. Paul,	do.	*Boston.*

Rev. Paul Cuffee, Presbyterian, *Long Island, State of New York*

Rev. Jacob Bishop, Baptist, *vicinity of Baltimore.*

A LIST

OF THE NAMES OF THE AFRICAN LOCAL PREACHERS OF THE AUTHOR'S ACQUAINTANCE.

Mr. Thomas Miller, sen.	Methodist,	*New York.*
Mr. Jacob Matthews,	do.	**do.**

....

Mr. George White,	Methodist,	*New York.*
Mr. Hanibal Moore,	do.	*Baltimore.*
Mr. Thomas Doublin,	do.	do.
Mr. Richard Williams,	do.	do.
Mr. James Coal,	do.	do.
Mr. Thomas Hall,	do.	do.
Mr. John Wigh,	do.	do.
Mr. Abner Coker,	do.	do.
Mr. George Martin,	do.	*Annapolis.*

......

A LIST OF AFRICAN CHURCHES.

2 Methodist, in Philadelphia.
1 Protestant, in   do.
1 Methodist, in New York.
1 Baptist, in   do.
1 Methodist, on Long Island in the state of New York.
1 Presbyterian, in New York.
1 Baptist, in Boston.
1 Methodist in Salem, New Jersey.
1   do.   in West Chester near Philadelphia.
2   do.   in Baltimore.
1   do.   in Wilmington, Delaware.
1   do.   in Annapolis, Maryland.
1   do.   in Charleston, South Carolina.

15 Total.

Number of African Methodists in the United States, in 1809, 31884.

......

A LIST

OF THE NAMES OF THE DESCENDANTS OF THE
AFRICAN RACE, WHO HAVE GIVEN PROOFS
OF TALENTS.

Rev. Absalom Jones, in a sermon on the abolition
of the slave trade. First of January, 1808, in
Philadelphia.

Mr. Peter Williams, junr. in an oration on the
abolition of the slave trade. First of January,
1808, in New York.

Rev. James Varrick, in a sermon, on the same day
and on the same occasion, in New York.

Mr. Henry Sipkins, in an oration on the abolition
of the slave trade. Second of January, 1809,
in New York.

Mr. William Hamilton, in an address before the
New York African Society for mutual relief.
Second of January, 1809, in New York.

Rev. William Miller, in a sermon on the abolition
of the slave trade. First of January, 1810, in
New York.

....

Mr. Henry Johnson, in an oration on the abolition of the slave trade. First of January, 1810, in New York.

Mr. James Forten, a letter addressed to congress for the rights of his coloured brethren. Philadelphia.

FINIS.

NATHANIEL PAUL

An Address, Delivered on the Celebration
of the Abolition of Slavery,
in the State of New York, July 5, 1827

AN

ADDRESS,

DELIVERED ON THE CELEBRATION OF THE

ABOLITION OF SLAVERY,

IN THE STATE OF NEW-YORK,

JULY 5, 1827.

———

BY NATHANIEL PAUL,

PASTOR OF THE FIRST AFRICAN BAPTIST SOCIETY

IN THE CITY OF ALBANY.

Published by the Trustees for the benefit of said Society.

———

ALBANY :

PRINTED BY JOHN B. VAN STEENBERGH.

••••••••••••

1827.

ADDRESS.

Through the long lapse of ages, it has been common for nations to record whatever was peculiar or interesting in the course of their history. Thus when Heaven, provoked by the iniquities of man, has visited the earth with the pestilence which moves in darkness or destruction, that wasteth at noonday, and has swept from existence, by thousands, its numerous inhabitants ; or when the milder terms of mercy have been dispensed in rich abundance, and the goodness of God has crowned the efforts of any people with peace and prosperity ; they have been placed upon their annals, and handed down to future ages, both for their amusement and profit. And as the nations which have already passed away, have been careful to select the most important events, peculiar to themselves, and have recorded them for the good of the people that should succeed them, so will we place it upon our history ; and we will tell the good story to our children and to our children's children, down to the latest posterity, that on the *fourth day of July,* in the year of our Lord 1827, slavery was abolished in the state of New-York.

Seldom, if ever, was there an occasion which required a public acknowledgment, or that deserved to be retained with gratitude of heart to the all-wise disposer of events, more than the present on which we have assembled.

It is not the mere gratification of the pride of the

heart, or any vain ambitious notion, that has influenced us to make our appearance in the public streets of our city, or to assemble in the sanctuary of the Most High this morning; but we have met to offer our tribute of thanksgiving and praise to almighty God for his goodness; to retrace the acts and express our gratitude to our public benefactors, and to stimulate each other to the performance of every good and virtuous act, which now does, or hereafter may devolve as a duty upon us, as freemen and citizens, in common with the rest of community.

And if ever it were necessary for me to offer an apology to an audience for my absolute inability to perform a task assigned me, I feel that the present is the period. However, relying, for support on the hand of Him who has said, "I will never leave nor forsake;" and confiding in your charity for every necessary allowance, I venture to engage in the arduous undertaking.

In contemplating the subject before us, in connection with the means by which so glorious an event has been accomplished, we find much which requires our deep humiliation and our most exalted praises. We are permitted to behold one of the most pernicious and abominable of all enterprises, in which the depravity of human nature ever led man to engage, entirely eradicated. The power of the tyrant is subdued, the heart of the oppressed is cheered liberty is proclaimed to the captive, and the opening of the prison to those who were bound, and he who had long been the miserable victim of cruelty and degradation, is elevated to the common rank in which our benevolent Creator first designed, that man should move,—all of which have been effected by means the most simple, yet perfectly efficient: Not by those fearful judgments of the almighty, which have so often fell upon the different parts of the earth; which have overturned nations and kingdoms; scattered thrones and sceptres; nor is the glory of the achievement, tarnished with the horrors of the field of battle. We hear not the cries of the widow and the fatherless; nor are our hearts affected with the sight of garments rolled in blood; but all has been done by the diffusion and influence of the pure, yet powerful principles of benevolence, before which the pitiful impotency of tyranny and oppression, is scattered and dispersed, like the chaff before the rage of the whirlwind.

I will not, on this occasion, attempt fully to detail the abominations of the traffic to which we have already alluded. Slavery, with its concomitants and consequences, in the best attire in which it can possibly be presented, is but a hateful monster, the very demon of avarice and oppression, from its first introduction to the present time; it has been among all nations the scourge of heaven, and the curse of the earth. It is so contrary to the laws which the God of nature has laid down as the rule of action by which the conduct of man is to be regulated towards his fellow man, which binds him to love his neighbour as himself, that it ever has, and ever will meet the decided disapprobation of heaven.

In whatever form we behold it, its visage is satanic, its origin the very offspring of hell, and in all cases its effects are grevious.

On the shores of Africa, the horror of the scene commeuces; here, the merciless tyrant, divested of every thing human, except the form, begins the action. The laws of God and the tears of the oppressed are alike disregarded ; and with more than savage barbarity, husbands and wives, parents and children, are parted to meet no more: and, if not doomed to an untimely death, while on the passage, yet are they for life consigned to a captivity still more terrible; a captivity, at the very thought of which, every heart, not already biassed with unhallowed prejudices, or callous to every tender impression, pauses and revolts; exposed to the caprice of those whose tender mercies are cruel ; unprotected by the laws of the land, and doomed to drag out miserable existence, without the remotest shadow of a hope of deliverence, until the king of terrors shall have executed his office, and consigned them to the kinder slumbers of death. But its pernicious tendency may be traced still farther: not only are its effects of the most disastrous character, in relation to the slave, but it extends its influence to the slave holder; and in many instances it is hard to say which is most wretched, the slave or the master.

After the fall of man, it would seem that God, foreseeing that pride and arrogance would be the necessary consequences of the apostacy, and that man would seek to usurp undue authority over his fellow, wisely ordained that he should obtain his bread by the sweat of his brow ; but con-

trary to this sacred mandate of heaven, slavery has
been introduced, supporting the one in all the absurd luxuries of life, at the expense of the liberty
and independence of the other.   Point me to any
section of the earth where slavery, to any considerable extent exists, and I will point you to a people
whose morals are corrupted ; and when pride, vanity and profusion are permitted to range unrestrained in all their desolating effects, and thereby idle-
ness and luxury are promoted, under the influence of
which, man, becoming insensible of his duty to his
God and his fellow creature ; and indulging in all the
pride and vanity of his own heart, says to his soul,
thou hast much goods laid up for many years.   But
while thus sporting, can it be done with impunity ?
Has conscience ceased to be active ? Are there no
forebodings of a future day of punishment, and of
meeting the merited avenger ? Can he retire after
the business of the day and repose in safety? Let
the guards around his mansion, the barred doors of
his sleeping room, and the loaded instruments of
death beneath his pillow, answer the question.—
And if this were all, it would become us, perhaps, to
cease to murmur, and bow in silent submission to
that providence which had ordained this present
state of existence, to be but a life of degradation and
suffering.

Since affliction is but the common lot of men, this
life, at best, is but a vapor that ariseth and soon pas-
seth away. Man, said the inspired sage, that is born
of a woman, is of few days and full of trouble ; and
in a certain sense, it is not material what our pre-

sent situation may be, for short is the period that humbles all to the dust, and places the monarch and the beggar, the slave and the master, upon equal thrones. But although this life is short, and attended with one entire scene of anxious perplexity, and few and evil are the days of our pilgrimage; yet man is advancing to another state of existence, bounded only by the vast duration of eternity! in which happiness or misery await us all. The great author of our existence has marked out the way that leads to the glories of the upper world, and through the redemption which is in Christ Jesus, salvation is offered to all. But slavery forbids even the approach of mercy; it stands as a barrier in the way to ward off the influence of divine grace; it shuts up the avenues of the soul, and prevents its receiving divine instruction; and scarce does it permit its miserable captives to know that there is a God, a Heaven or a Hell!

Its more than detestable picture has been attempted to be portrayed by the learned, and the wise, but all have fallen short, and acknowledged their inadequacy to the task, and have been compelled to submit, by merely giving an imperfect shadow of its reality. Even the immortal Wilberforce, a name that can never die while Africa lives, after exerting his ingenuity, and exhausting the strength of his masterly mind, resigns the effort, and calmly submits by saying, " never was there, indeed, a system so replete with wickedness and cruelty to whatever part of it we turn our eyes; we could find no comfort, no satisfaction, no relief. It was the gracious ordinance of providence, both in the natural and moral world, that good should often arise out of evil. Hurricanes clear the air; and the propagation of truth was promoted by persecution, pride, vanity, and profusion contributed often, in their remoter consequences, to the happiness of mankind. In common, what was in itself evil and vicious, was permitted to carry along with it some circumstances of palliation. The Arab was hospitable, the robber brave; we did not necessarily find cruelty associated with fraud or meanness with injustice. But here the case was far otherwise. It was the prerogative of this detestable traffic, to separate from evil its concomitant good, and to reconcile discordant mischief. It robbed war of its generosity, it deprived peace of its security. We saw in it the vices of polished society, without its knowledge or its comforts, and the evils of barbarism without its simplicity; no age, no sex, no rank, no condition, was exempt from the fatal influence of this wide wasting calamity. Thus it attained to the fullest measure of its pure, unmixed, unsophisticated wickedness; and scorning all competition or comparison, it stood without a rival in the secure and undisputed possession of its detestable pre-eminence.

Such were the views which this truly great and good man, together with his fellow philanthropists, took of this subject, and such are the strong terms in which he has seen fit to express his utter abhorrence of its origin and effects. Thus have we hinted at some of the miseries connected with slavery. And while I turn my thoughts back and survey what is past, I see our forefathers seized by the hand of the rude ruffian, and torn from their native homes and all that they held dear or sacred. I follow them down the lonesome way, until I see each safely placed on board the gloomy slave ship ; I hear the passive groan, and the clanking of the chains which bind them. I see the tears which follow each other in quick succession adown the dusky cheek.

I view them casting the last and longing look towards the land which gave them birth, until at length the ponderous anchor is weighed, and the canvass spread to catch the favored breeze; I view them wafted onward until they arrive at the destined port; I behold those who have been so unfortunate as to survive the passage, emerging from their loathsome prison, and landing amidst the noisy rattling of the massy fetters which confine them; I see the crowd of trafficers in human flesh gathering, each anxious to seize the favored opportunity of enriching himself with their toils, their tears and their blood. I view them doomed to the most abject state of degraded misery, and exposed to suffer all that unrestrained tyranny can inflict, or that human nature is capable of sustaining.

Tell me, ye mighty waters, why did ye sustain the ponderous load of misery ? or speak, ye winds, and say why it was that ye executed your office to waft them onward to the still more dismal state ; and ye proud waves, why did you refuse to lend your aid and to have overwhelmed them with your billows ? Then should they have slept sweetly in the bosom of the great deep, and so have been hid from sorrow. And, oh thou immaculate God, be not angry with us,

while we come into this thy sanctuary, and make
the bold inquiry in this thy holy temple, why it was
that thou didst look on with the calm indifference
of an unconcerned spectator, when thy holy law
was violated, thy divine authority despised and a
portion of thine own creatures reduced to a state
of mere vassalage and misery? Hark! while he an-
swers from on high: hear him proclaiming from the
skies—Be still, and know that I am God! Clouds
and darkness are round about me; yet righteousness and judgment are the habitation of my throne.
I do my will and pleasure in the heavens above, and
in the earth beneath; it is my sovereign prerogative to bring good out of evil, and cause the wrath of
man to praise me, and the remainder of that wrath
I will restrain.

Strange, indeed, is the idea, that such a system,
fraught with such consummate wickedness, should
ever have found a place in this the otherwise happiest of all countries.——a country, the very soil of
which is said to be consecrated to liberty, and its
fruits the equal rights of man. But strange as the
idea may seem, or paradoxical as it may appear to
those acquainted with the constitution of the government, or who have read the bold declaration of
this nation's independence; yet it is a fact that can
neither be denied or controverted, that in the United States of America, at the expiration of fifty
years after its becoming a free and independent nation, there are no less than fifteen hundred thousand
human beings still in a state of unconditional vassalage.

Yet America is first in the profession of the love of liberty, and loudest in proclaiming liberal sentiments towards all other nations, and feels herself insulted, to be branded with any thing bearing the appearance of tyranny or oppression. Such are the palpable inconsistencies that abound among us and such is the medley of contradictions which stain the national character, and renders the American republic a by-word, even among despotic nations. But while we pause and wonder at the contradictory sentiments held forth by the nation, and contrast its profession and practice, we are happy to have it in our power to render an apology for the existence of the evil, and to offer an excuse for the framers of the constitution. It was before the sons of Columbia felt the yoke of their oppressors, and rose in their strength to put it off that this land become contaminated with slavery. Had this not been the case, led by the spirit of pure republicanism, that then possessed the souls of those patriots who were struggling for liberty, this soil would have been sufficiently guarded against its intrusion, and the people of these United States to this day, would have been strangers to so great a curse. It was by the permission of the British parliament, that the human species first became an article of merchandize among them, and as they were accessary to its introduction, it well becomes them to be first, as a nation, in arresting its progress and effecting its expulsion. It was the immortal Clarkson, a name that will be associated with all that is sublime in

mercy, until the final consummation of all things,
who first looking abroad, beheld the sufferings of
Africa, and looking at home, he saw his country
stained with her blood. He threw aside the vest-
ments of the priesthood, and consecrated himself to
the holy purpose of rescuing a continent from ra-
pine and murder, and of erasing this one sin from
the book of his nation's iniquities. Many wer• the
difficulties to be encountered, many were the hardships to be endured, many were the persecutions to
be met with; formidable, indeed, was the opposing
party. The sensibility of the slave merchants and
planters was raised to the highest pitch of resent-
ment. Influenced by the love of money, every scheme
was devised, every measure was adopted, every
plan was executed, that might throw the least barrier in the way of the holy cause of the abolition of
this traffic. The consequences of such a measure
were placed in the most appalling light that ingen-
ious falsehood could invent; the destruction of commerce, the ruin of the merchants, the rebellion of
the slaves, the massacre of the planters, were all
artfully and fancifully pictured, and reduced to a
certainty in the minds of many of the members of
parliament, and a large proportion of the community. But the cause of justice and humanity were
not to be deserted by him and his fellow philanthropists, on account of difficulties. We have seen them
for twenty years persevering against all opposition,
and surmounting every obstacle they found in their
way. Nor did they relax aught of their exertions,

until the cries of the oppressed having roused the
sensibility of the nation, the island empress rose in
her strength, and said to this foul traffic, "thus far
hast thou gone, but thou shalt go no farther." Happy for us, my brethren, that the principles of benevolence were not exclusively confined to the isle of
Great Britain. There have lived, and there still
do live, men in this country, who are patriots and
philanthropists, not merely in name, but in heart and
practice ; men whose compassions have long since
led them to pity the poor and despised sons of Africa. They have heard their groans, and have seen
their blood, and have looked with an holy indignation upon the oppressor: nor was there any thing
wanting except the power to have crushed the tyrant and liberated the captive. Through their in-
strumentality, the blessings of freedom have long
since been enjoyed by all classes of people throughout New-England, and through their influence, under the Almighty, we are enabled to recognize the
fourth day of the present month, as the day in which
the cause of justice and humanity have triumphed
over tyranny and oppression, and slavery is forever
banished from the state of New York.

Among the many who have vindicated the cause
of the oppressed, within the limits of this state, we
are proud to mention the names of Eddy and Murray, of Jay and Tompkins, who, together with their
fellow philanthropists embarked in the holy cause of
emancipation, with a zeal which well expressed
the sentiments of their hearts. They proved themselves to be inflexible against scorn, persecution,

and contempt; and although all did not live to see
the conflict ended, yet their survivors never relaxed
their exertions until the glorious year of 1817, when,
by the wise and patriotic legislature of this state, a
law was passed for its final extirpation. We will
mourn for those who are gone, we will honour those
who survive, until time extinguishes the lamp of
their existence. When dead, they shall still
live in our memory ; we will follow them to their
tombs, we will wet their graves with our tears; and
upon the heart of every descendant of Africa, their
deeds shall be written, and their names shall vi-
brate sweetly from ear to ear, down to the latest
posterity. From what has already taken place, we
are encouraged to expect still greater things. We
look forward with pleasing anticipation to that period, when it shall no longer be said that in a land
of freemen there are men in bondage, but when
this foul stain will be entirely erased, and this,
worst of evils, will be forever done away. The progress of emancipation, though slow, is nevertheless
certain : It is certain, because that God who has
made of one blood all nations of men, and who is
said to be no respecter of persons, has so decreed ;
I therefore have no hesitation in declaring from this
sacred place, that not only throughout the United
States of America, but throughout every part of the
habitable world where slavery exists, it will be a-
bolished. However grea t may be the opposition of
those who are supported by the traffic, yet slavery
will cease. The lordly planter who has his thousands
in bondage, may stretch himself upon his couch of

ivory, and sneer at the exertions which are made by
the humane and benevolent, or he may take his
stand upon the floor of Congress, and mock the pitiful generosity of the east or west for daring to med-
dle with the subject, and attempting to expose its
injustice : he may threaten to resist all efforts for a
general or a partial emancipation even to a dissolution of the union.   But still I declare that slavery
will be extinct; a universal and not a partial emancipation must take place ; nor is the period far distant.
The indefatigable exertions of the philantrophists in
England to have it abolished in their West India
Islands, the recent revolutions in South America,
the catastrophe and exchange of power in the Isle
of Hayti, the restless disposition of both master and
slave in the southern states, the constitution of
our government, the effects of literary and moral instruction, the generous feelings of the pious and benevolent, the influence and spread of the holy religion of the cross of Christ, and the irrevocable de-
crees of Almighty God, all combine their efforts,
and with united voice declare, that the power of
tyranny must be subdued, the captive must be liberated, the oppressed go free, and slavery must
revert back to its original chaos of darkness, and
be forever annihilated from the earth.   Did I believe that it would always continue, and that man
to the end of time would be permitted with impunity to usurp the same undue authority over his fellow,
I would disallow any allegiance or obligation I was
under to my fellow creatures, or any submission
that I owed to the laws of my country ; I would deny

the superintending power of divine providence in
the affairs of this life; I would ridicule the religion
of the Saviour of the world, and treat as the worst of
men the ministers of the everlasting gospel; I would
consider my Bible as a book of false and delusive fa-
bles, and commit it to the flames ; nay, I would still
go farther; I would at once confess myself an atheist,
and deny the existence of a holy God.

But slavery will cease, and the equal rights of man
will be universally acknowledged. Nor is its tardy
progress any argument against its final accomplish-
ment. But do I hear it loudly responded,—this is
but a mere wild fanaticism, or at best but the mis-
guided conjecture of an untutored descendant of
Africa. Be it so. I confess my ignorance, and bow
with due deference to my superiors in understanding; but if in this case I err, the error is not peculiar
to myself ; if I wander, I wander in a region of light
from whose political hemisphere the sun of liberty
pours forth his refulgent rays, around which dazzle
the star like countenances of Clarkson, Wilberforce,
Pitt, Fox and Grenville, Washington, Adams, Jefferson, Hancock and Franklin ; if I err, it is their
sentiments that have caused me to stray. For
these are the doctrines which they taught while
with us; nor can we reasonably expect that since
they have entered the unbounded space of eternity,
and have learned more familiarly the perfections of
that God who governs all things that their sentiments have altered. Could they now come forth
among us, they would tell that what they have
learned in the world of spirits, has served only to

confirm what they taught while here; they would
tell us, that all things are rolling on according to
the sovereign appointment of the eternal Jehovah,
who will overturn and overturn until he whose right
it is to reign, shall come and the period will be ush-
ered in; when the inhabitants of the earth will
learn by experience what they are now slow to believe.—that our God is a God of justice, and no
respecter of persons. But while, on the one hand,
we look back and rejoice at what has already taken
place, and on the other, we look forward with pleasure to that period when men will be respected according to their characters, and not according to
their complexion, and when their vices alone will
render them contemptible; while we rejoice at the
thought of this land's becoming a land of freemen,
we pause, we reflect. What, we would ask, is liberty
without virtue? It tends to lasciviousness; and
what is freedom but a curse, and even destruction, to
the profligate? Not more desolating in its effects is the
mountain torrent, breaking from its lofty confines and
rushing with vast impetuosity upon the plains beneath, marring as it advances all that is lovely
in the works of nature and of art, than the votaries of
vice and immorality, when permitted to range unrestrained.   Brethren, we have been called into liberty; only let us use that liberty as not abu-
sing it. This day commences a new era in our history; new scenes, new prospects, open before us, and
it follows as a necessary consequence, that new duties devolve upon us; duties, which if properly attended to, cannot fail to improve our moral condition,

and elevate us to a rank of respectable standing
with the community; or if neglected, we fall at once
into the abyss of contemptible wretchedness : It is
righteousness alone that exalteth a nation, and sin
is a reproach to any people. Our liberties, says Mr.
Jefferson, are the gift of God, and they are not to be
violated but with his wrath. Nations and individuals have been blest of the Almighty in proportion to
the manner in which they have appreciated the mercies conferred upon them : an abuse of his goodness
has always incured his righteous frown while a right
improvement of his beneficence has secured and
perpetuated his gracious smiles : an abuse of his
goodness has caused those fearful judgments which
have destroyed cities, demolished thrones, overturned empires, and humbled to the dust, the proud-
est and most exalted of nations. As a confirmation
of which, the ruinous heaps of Egypt, Tyre, Babylon, and Jerusalem, stand as everlasting monuments
If we would then answer the great design of our creation, and glorify the God who has made us ; if we
would avert the judgment of Heaven; if we would
honor our public benefactors ; if we would counter-
act the designs of our enemies ; if we would have
our own blessings perpetuated, and secure the happiness of our children and our children's children,
let each come forward and act well his part, in
whatever circle he may move, or in whatever station he may fill; let the fear of God and the good of
our fellow men, be the governing principles of the
heart. We do well to remember, that every act of
ours is more or less connected with the general

cause of the people of colour, and with the general cause of emancipation. Our conduct has an important bearing, not only on those who are yet in bondage in this country, but its influence is extended to the isles of India, and to every part of the world where the abomination of slavery is known. Let us then relieve ourselves from the odious stigma which some have long since cast upon us. that we were incapacitated by the God of nature, for the enjoyment of the rights of freemen, and convince them and the world that although our complexion may differ, yet we have hearts susceptible of feeling; judgment capable of discerning. and prudence sufficient to manage our affairs with discretion, and by example prove ourselves worthy the blessings we enjoy.— That it is the duty of all rational creatures to consult the interest of their species, is a fact against which there can be no reasonable objection. It is recorded to the honour of Titus, who perhaps was the most benevolent of all the Roman emperors : on recollecting one evening that he had done nothing the day preceding, beneficial to mankind, the monarch exclaimed, "I have lost a day." The wide field of usefulness is now open before us, and we are called upon by every consideration of duty which we owe to our God, to ourselves, to our children, and to our fellow-creatures generally, to enter with a fixed determination to act well our part, and labour to promote the happiness and welfare of all.

There remains much to be done, and there is much to encourage us to action. The foundation for literary, moral and religious improvement, we trust, is already laid in the formation of the public and private schools, for the instruction of our children, together with the churches of different denominations already established. From these institutions we are encouraged to expect the happiest results; and while many of us are passing down the declivity of life, and fast hastening to the grave, how animating the thought that the rising generation is advancing under more favourable auspicies than we were permitted to enjoy, soon to fill the places we now occupy; and in relation to them vast is the responsibility that rests upon us; much of their future usefulness depends upon the discharge of the duties we owe them. They are advancing, not to fill the place of slaves, but of freemen: and in order to fill such a station with honor to themselves, and with good to the public, how necessary their education, how important the moral and religious cultivation of their minds! Blessed be God, we live in a day that our fathers desired to see, but died without the sight: a day in which science, like the sun of the firmament, rising, darting as he advances his beams to every quarter of the globe. The mists and darkness scatter at his approach, and all nations and people are blessed with his rays; so the glorious light of science is spreading from east to west, and Afric's sons are catching the glance of its beams as it passes; its enlightening rays scatter the mists of moral darkness and ignorance which have but too long overshadowed their minds; it enlightens the understanding, directs the thoughts of the heart, and is calculated to influence the soul to the performance of every good and virtuous act. The

God of Nature has endowed our children with intellectual powers surpassed by none; nor is there any thing wanting but their careful cultivation, in order to fit them for stations the most honorable, sacred, or useful. And may we not, without becoming vain in our imaginations, indulge the pleasing anticipation, that within the little circle of those connected with our families, there may hereafter be found the scholar, the statesman, or the herald of the cross of Christ: Is it too much to say, that among that little number there shall yet be one found like to the wise legislator of Israel, who shall take his brethren by the hand, and lead them forth from worse than Egyptian bondage, to the happy Canaan of civil and religious liberty; or one whose devotedness towards the cause of God, and whose zeal for the salvation of Africa, shall cause him to leave the land which gave him birth, and cross the Atlantic, eager to plant the standard of the cross upon every hill of that vast continent, that has hitherto ignobly submitted to the baleful crescent, or crouched under the iron bondage of the vilest superstition. Our prospects brighten as we pursue the subject, and we are encouraged to look forward to that period when the moral desert of Africa shall submit to cultivation, and verdant groves and fertile vallies, watered by the streams of Siloia, shall meet the eye that has long surveyed only the wide spread desolations of slavery, despotism, and death. How changed shall then be the aspect of the moral and political world! Africa, elevated to more than her original dignity, and redressed for the many aggravated and complicated wrongs she has sustained, with her emancipated sons, shall take her place among the other nations of the earth. The iron manacles of slavery shall give place to the still stronger bonds of brotherly love and affection, and justice and equity shall be the governing principles that shall regulate the conduct of men of every nation. Influenced by such motives, encouraged by such prospects, let us enter the field with a fixed determination to live and to die in the holy cause.

Names of the Senators who voted for the Law, in 1817.

DANIEL D. TOMPKINS, Governor.
JOHN TAYLER, Lt. Governor.

Mr. Allen,	Mr. Hascall,	Mr. Ross,
„ Becknell,	„ Hart,	„ Seymour,
„ Bloom,	„ Keyes,	„ Stewart,
„ Bowne,	„ Knox,	„ Tibbits,
„ Cantine,	„ Livingston,	„ Van Buren,
„ Crosby,	„ Noyes,	„ Van Vechten.
„ Ditmis,	„ Ogden,	20

Names of the Members of Assembly who voted for the Law, in 1817.

Mr. Albert,	Mr. Ganson,	Mr. Pettit,
„ Ambler,	„ A. Green,	„ Platt,
„ Arnold,	„ B. Green,	„ Rochester,
„ Barnes,	„ Gross,	„ Roseburgh,
„ Barstow,	„ Hamilton,	„ Russell,
„ Beach,	„ Hammond,	„ Sanford,
„ Beckwith,	„ Heeney,	„ Sargent,
„ Benton,	„ Hopkins,	„ E. Smith,
„ Brown,	„ Hubbard,	„ I. Smith,
„ Camp,	„ Keeler,	„ R. Smith,
„ Campbell,	„ Kissam,	„ S. A. Smith,
„ Carll,	„ Lee,	„ Squire,
„ Carpenter,	„ McFadden,	„ Stebbins,
„ Child	„ Mann,	„ Thompson,
„ Concklin,	„ Marsh,	„ Townsend,
„ Cook,	„ Miles,	„ Turner,
„ Day,	„ G. Miller,	„ Wakely,
„ Doty,	„ I. Miller,	„ Walbridge,
„ Duer,	„ Mooers,	„ Warner,
„ Eldridge,	„ Mott,	„ Webb,
„ Faulkner,	„ Noble,	„ Webster,
„ Finch,	„ Olmstead,	„ White,
„ Ford,	„ Paine,	„ I. Whitney,
„ Gale,	„ Palmer,	„ Wilcoxson,
„ Gansevoort,	„ Parsons,	„ Wood. 75

HYMN.

Tune—"*Van Halls' Hymn.*"

AFRIC'S sons, awake, rejoice !
To you this day sounds freedom's voice ;
This day to us our birthright's given;
United raise your thanks to heaven.

May every son, with grateful heart,
This day from others set apart :
The hour that first proclaim'd us free,
Shall be our lasting jubilee.

When history unrols her page
Of Africa's degraded age,
Then shall the dawn of freedom's light
A radiance shed o'er slavery's night.

Come, raise your thankful voice to Heaven ;
To us Religion's truths are given ;
In lands where late the heathen trod,
Now Ethiopia seeks her God.

O! may he guide our rugged way ;
Our flame by night, our cloud by day ;
Our injuries let all forgive,
And by the gospel's precepts live.

WILLIAM HAMILTON

*Address to the Fourth Annual Convention
of the People of Color of the United States*

ADDRESS

TO THE

FOURTH ANNUAL CONVENTION

OF THE

FREE PEOPLE OF COLOR

OF THE

UNITED STATES.

**DELIVERED AT THE OPENING OF THEIR SESSION IN THE
CITY OF NEW-YORK, JUNE 2, 1834.**

By WILLIAM HAMILTON, Sen.
PRESIDENT OF THE CONVENTIONAL BOARD.

NEW-YORK:
S. W. BENEDICT & CO. PRINTERS, 162 NASSAU ST.
1834.

ADDRESS.

Gentlemen:

It is with the most pleasing sensations, and feelings of high gratification, that I, in behalf of my colored fellow citizens of New York, tender you of the delegation to this convention a hearty welcome to our city. And in behalf of the conventional board, I repeat the welcome. And, gentlemen, with regard to myself, my full heart vibrates the felicitation.

You have convened to take into consideration what may be the best means for the promotion of the best interest of the people of color of these United States, particularly of the free people thereof.

And that such convention is highly necessary, I think a few considerations will amply show.

First, the present form of society divides the interest of the community into several parts. Of these, there is that of the white man, that of the slave, and that of the free colored man. How lamentable, how very lamentable it is that there should be, any where on earth, a community of castes, with separate interests! That society must be the most happy, where the good of one is the common good of the whole. Civilization is not perfect, nor has reason full sway, until the community shall see that a wrong done to one is a wrong done to the whole; that the interest of one is or ought to be the common interest of the whole. Surely that must be a happy state of society where the sympathies of all are to all alike.

How pleasing, what a compliment to the nation, is the expression of Mons. Vallier a celebrated traveler in Africa, where speaking of the Hottentots, he says "There none need to offer themselves as objects of compassion, for all are compassionate." Whatever our early-tutored prejudice may say to the contrary, such a people must be happy. Give me a residence in such a society, and I shall fancy myself in a community the most refined.

But alas for the people of color in this community! their interest is not identified with that of other men. From them, white men stand aloof. For them the eye of pity hath scarcely a tear.

To them the hand of kindness is palsied, to them the dregs of mercy scarcely are given. To them the finger of scorn is pointed; contumely and reproach is continually theirs. They are a taunt, a hissing, and a by-word. They must cringe, and crouch, and crawl, and succumb to their peers. Long, long, long has the demon of prejudice and persecution beset their path. And must they make no effort to throw off the evils by which they are beset? Ought they not to meet to spread out their wrongs before one another? Ought they not to meet to consult on the best means of relief? Ought they not to make one weak effort; nay, one strong, one mighty moral effort, to roll off the burden that crushes them?

Under present circumstances it is highly necessary the free people of color should combine, and closely attend to their own particular interest. All kinds of jealousy should be swept away from among them, and their whole eye fixed, intently fixed on their own peculiar welfare. And can they do better than to meet thus; to take into consideration what are the best means to promote their elevation, and after having decided, to pursue those means with unabating zeal until their end is obtained?

Another reason why this convention is necessary, is, that there is formed a strong combination against the people of color, by some who are

5

the master spirits of the day, by men whose influence is of the strongest character, to whom this nation bow in humble submission, and submit to their superior judgment, who turn public sentiment which ever way they please.

You cannot but perceive that I allude to the Colonization Society. However pure the motives of some of the members of that society may be, yet the master spirits thereof are evil minded towards us. They have put on the garb of angels of light. Fold back their covering, and you have in full array those of darkness.

I need not spread before you the proofs of their evil purposes. Of that you have had a quantity sufficient; and were there no other good reason for this convention, the bare circumstance of the existence of such an institution would be a sufficient one. I do hope, confidently hope, that the time will arrive, and is near at hand, when we shall be in full possession of all the rights of men.

But as long at least as the Colonization Society exists, will a convention of colored people be highly necessary. This society is the great Dagon of the land, before whom the people bow and cry, Great Jehovah, and to whom they would sacrifice the free people of color. That society has spread itself over this whole land, it is artful, it suits itself to all places. It is one thing at the south, and another at the north; it blows hot and cold; it sends forth bitter and sweet; it sometimes represents us as the most corrupt, vicious, and abandoned of any class of men in the community. Then again we are kind, meek, and gentle. Here we are ignorant, idle, a nuisance, and a drawback on the resources of the country. But as abandoned as we are, in Africa we shall civilize and christianize all that heathen country.

And by thus preaching continually, they have distilled into the minds of the community a desire to see us removed.

They have resorted to every artifice to effect their purposes.

By exciting in the minds of the white community the fears of insurrection and amalgamation;

By petitioning state legislatures to grant us no favors;

By petitioning congress to aid in sending us away;

By using their influence to prevent the establishment of seminaries for our instruction in the higher branches of education.

And such are the men of that society that the community are blind to their absurdities, contradictions, and paradoxes. They are well acquainted with the ground and the wiles by which to beguile the people.

It is therefore highly necessary we should meet, in order that we may confer on the best means to frustrate the purpose of so awful a foe.

I would beg leave to recommend an attentive consideration to this matter. Already you have done much toward the enervation of this giant: he begins to grow feeble; indeed he seems to be making his last struggle, if we may judge from his recent movements. Hang around him; assail him quickly. He is vulnerable. Well pointed darts will fetch him down, and soon he breathes no more.

Cheer up, my friends! Already has your protest against the Colonizaiton Society shown to the world that the people of color are not willing to be expatriated. Cheer up. Already a right feeling begins to prevail. The friends of justice, of humanity, and the rights of man are drawing rapidly together, and are forming a moral phalanx in your defence.

That hitherto strong-footed, but sore-eyed vixen, prejudice, is limping off, seeking the shade. The Anti-Slavery Society and the friends of immediate abolition, are taking a noble, bold, and manly stand, in the cause of universal liberty. It is true they are assailed on every quarter, but the more they are assailed the faster they recruit. From present appearances the prospect is cheering, in a high degree. Anti-Slavery Societies are forming in every direction.

Next August proclaims the British dominions free from slaves.

These United states are her children, they will soon follow so good an example. Slavery, that Satanic monster, that beast whose mark has been so long stamped on the forehead of the nations, shall be chained and cast down into blackness and darkness forever.

Soon, my brethren, shall the judgment be set. Then shall rise in glory and triumph, reason, virtue, kindness and liberty, and take a high exalted stand among the sons of men. Then shall tyranny, cruelty, prejudice and slavery be cast down to the lowest depths of oblivion ; yea, be banished from the presence of God, and the glory of his power forever. Oh blessed consummation, and devoutly to be desired !

It is for you, my brethren, to help on in this work of moral improvement. Man is capable of high advances in his reasoning and moral faculties. Man is in the pursuit of happiness. And reason, or experience, which is the parent of reason, tells us that the highest state of morality is the highest state of happiness. Aside from a future day of judgment and retribution, there is always a day of retribution at hand. That society is most miserable that is most immoral—that most happy that is most virtuous. Let me therefore recommend earnestly that you press upon our people the necessity and advantage of a moral reformation. It may not produce an excess of riches, but it will produce a higher state of happiness, and render our circumstances easier.

You, gentlemen, can begin here. By managing this conference in a spirit of good will and true politeness ; by constantly keeping in view and cultivating a spirit of peace, order and harmony, rather than satire, wit, and eloquence ; by putting the best possible construction on each other's language, rather than charging each other with improper motives.

'These dispositions will bespeak our character more or less virtuous and refined, and render our sitting more or less pleasant. I will only now add, that the report of the conventional board will be submitted at your call; and my earnest hope is that you may have a peaceful, pleasant sitting.

HOSEA EASTON

A Treatise on the Intellectual Character,
and Civil and Political Condition
of the Colored People of the United States

A TREATISE

ON THE

INTELLECTUAL CHARACTER,

AND

CIVIL AND POLITICAL CONDITION

OF THE

COLORED PEOPLE OF THE U. STATES;

AND THE

PREJUDICE EXERCISED TOWARDS THEM:

WITH A SERMON

ON THE

DUTY OF THE CHURCH TO THEM.

BY REV. H. EASTON,
A COLORED MAN.

BOSTON:
PRINTED AND PUBLISHED BY ISAAC KNAPP.
1837.

PREFACE.

IT is with diffidence that I offer this treatise to the public; but an earnest desire to contribute my mite, for the benefit of my afflicted brethren, is my only apology. The subject is one of peculiar difficulty; especially as it is one in which I am deeply interested.

To speak or write on a subject relating to one's self, is peculiarly embarrassing; and especially so, under a deep sense of injury.

As an apology for the frequent errors that may occur in the following pages, I would remark: It cannot be reasonably expected, that a literary display could adorn the production of one from whom popular sentiment has withheld almost every advantage, even of a common education.

If this work should chance to fall into the hands of any whose minds are so sordid, and whose hearts are so inflexible, as to load it, with its author, with censure on that account merely, I would only say to them, that I shall not be disposed to envy them in the enjoyment of their sentiments, while I endeavor to content myself in the enjoyment of a consciousness of having done what I could to effect the establishment of righteousness and peace in the earth.

Hartford, Ct., March, 1837.

INTRODUCTION.

I conclude that, by this time, one great truth is acknowledged by all Christendom, viz.—God hath made of one blood all nations of men for to dwell on all the face of the earth. Or, in other words, I conclude it is a settled point with the wisest of the age, that no constitutional difference exists in the children of men, which can be said to be established by hereditary laws. If the proposition be granted, it will follow, that whatever differences exist, are casual or accidental. The variety of color, in the humun species, is the result of the same laws which variegate the whole creation. The same species of flowers is variegated with innumerable colors ; and yet the species is the same, possessing the same general qualities, undergoing no intrinsic change, from these accidental causes. So it is with the human species. These varieties are indispensable, for the distinction of different objects, throughout the whole range of creation.

The hair is subject to the same laws of variety with the skin, though it may be considered in a somewhat different light. Were I asked why my hair is curled, my answer would be, because God gave nature the gift of producing variety, and that gift, like uncontrolled power every where, was desirous to act like itself; and thus being influenced by some cause unknown to man, she turned out her work in the form of my hair ; and on being influenced by some other cause, she turned out hair of different texture, and gave it to another man. This would be the best answer I could give ; for it is impossible for man to comprehend nature or her works. She has been supplied with

an ability by her author to do wonders, insomuch that some
have been foolish enough to think her to be God. All must
confess she possesses a mysterious power to produce variety.
We need only visit the potato and corn patch, (not a costly
school,) and we shall be perfectly satisfied ; for there, in the
same hill, on one stalk, sprung from one potato, you may find
several of different colors ; and upon the same corn-stalk you
may find two ears, one white or yellow, and the other deep red ;
and sometimes you may find an astonishing variety of colors
displayed on one ear among the kernels ; and what makes the
observation more delightful, they are never found quarrelling
about their color, though some have shades of extreme beauty.
If you go to the field of grass, you will find that all grass is
the same grass in variety ; go to the herds and flocks, and among
the feathered tribe, or view nature where you will, she tells us
all that we can know, why it is that one man's head bears woolly,
and another flaxen hair.

But when we come to talk about intellectual differences, we
are brought into a new field of investigation. I call it a new or
another field, because I cannot believe that nature has any thing
to do in variegating intellect, any more than it has power over
the soul. Mind can act on matter, but matter cannot act upon
mind ; hence it fills an entirely different sphere ; therefore, we
must look for a cause of difference of intellect elsewhere, for it
cannot be found in nature. In looking for a cause, we have no
right to go above nor below the sphere which the mind occupies ;
we cannot rationally conceive the cause to originate with God,
nor in matter. Nature never goes out of her own limits to produce her works ; all of which are perfect so far as she is concerned, and most assuredly God's works are perfect ; hence,
whatever imperfections there are in the mind, must have originated within its own sphere. But the question is, what is the
cause and the manner it affects ? Originally there was no difference of intellect, either constitutional or casual. Man was
perfect, and therefore to him there was no exception. After he
fell, we immediately find a difference of mind. In Abel we
find characteristics of a noble soul, a prolific mind ; his under-

standing appears to have been but very little, if any, impaired by the fall. But in Cain we find quite the reverse. His mind appears to have been narrow—his understanding dark—having wrapped himself up in a covetous mantle as contemptible as his conduct was wicked.

Now I see no reason why the causes of difference do not exist in the fall—in the act of transgression ; for certain it is that the mind has since been subject to the influence of every species of evil, which must be a secondary cause to the existing effect. Or the subject may be viewed in the following light, viz. : evil and good exist in the world, and as the mind is influenced by the one or the other, so is the different effect produced thereby.

There is no truth more palpable than this, that the mind is capable of high cultivation ; and that the degree of culture depends entirely on the means or agents employed to that end. In a country, therefore, where public sentiment is formed in favor of improving the mind, whatever the object may be, whether to promote good or evil, the mind is influenced thereby. The practical exercise of the mind is essential also to improvement and growth, and is directed likewise by public sentiment.

Public sentiment is founded on the real or imaginary interests of parties, whose individual interests are identified one with another. Public sentiment itself is directed in the exercise of its influence, by incidental circumstances, either local or foreign. In this current the mind is borne along, and at the instance of every change of event, is called to a new exercise of thought, conclusions, purposes, &c. ; whereas, had it not been for the change, there would have been no action produced in the mind : for it is manifest, that the sphere which mankind are destined to fill, is surrounded with a great variety of acting laws, which, were it not for such causes, would make their minds entirely passive ; but, under the influence of those causes, they are made to act not from constraint, but in accordance with an innate desire to avail themselves of collateral aid to their operations. It is manifest, therefore, that the more varying or complex the state of a people is incidentally rendered, the more power there is extant to call up renewed energies of the mind, the direct tendency of which is to confirm and strengthen it. Hence I deem it a fair conclusion, that whatever differences there are in the power of the intellect of nations, they are owing to the difference existing in the casual laws by which they are influenced. By consulting the history of nations, it may be seen that their genius perfectly accords with their habits of life, and the general maxims of their country; and that these habits and maxims possess a sameness of character with the incidental circumstances in which they originated.

As the intellect of a particular class will be in part the subject of this treatise, I wish in this place to follow the investigation of national difference of intellect, with its cause, by comparing the history of Europe and Africa.

Ham was the son of Noah, and founder of the African race, and progenitor to Assur, who probably founded the first government after the flood. It is evident from the best authority extant, that the arts and sciences flourished among this branch of the great family of man, long before its benefits were known to any other. History is explicit with regard to their hospitality also. At an early period of the existence of the government of Egypt, and while Chederlaomer, king of the Elamites, had already commenced the practice of robbery and bloodshed, Abraham was obliged by a famine to leave Canaan, where God had commanded him to settle, and to go into Egypt. ' This journey,' says a historian, ' gives occasion for Moses to mention some particulars with regard to the Egyptians ; and every stroke discovers the character of an improved and powerful nation. The Egyptian monarch, and the grandeur of his court, are described in the most glowing colors ;—and Ham, who led the colony into Egypt, has become the founder of a mighty empire. We are not, however, to imagine, that all the laws which took place in Egypt, and which have been so justly admired for their wisdom, were the work of this early age. Diodorus Siculus, a Greek writer, mentions many successive princes, who labored for their establishment and perfection. But in the time of Jacob, first principles of civil government seem to have been tolerably understood among the Egyptians. The country was divided into several districts or separate departments ; councils, composed of experienced and select persons, were established for the management of public affairs ; granaries for preserving corn were erected; and, in fine, the Egyptians in this age enjoyed a commerce far from inconsiderable. These facts, though of an ancient date, deserve our particular attention. It is from the Egyptians, that many of the arts, both of elegance and ability, have been handed down in an uninterrupted chain, to modern nations of Europe. The Egyptians communicated their arts to the Greeks ; the Greeks taught the Romans many improvements, both in the arts of peace and war ; and to the Romans, the present inhabitants of Europe are indebted for their civility and refinement.'

This noble people were not content with the enjoyment of luxury and ease, to the exclusion of their neighbors. At an early period they are found carrying the blessings of civilization into Greece ; and, although repulsed in their first attempt by the rude barbarity of the Greeks, yet their philanthropy soon inspired them to resume the enterprise, which resulted in the settlement of two colonies, one in Argos, and the other in Attica. The founders of these colonies succeeded in their endeavors to unite the wandering Greeks, which laid a foundation for the instructions they afterwards gave them. Sesostris, a prince of wonderful ability, is supposed to mount the throne of Egypt about 2341 years before Christ. Egypt in his time, it is said, was in all probability the most powerful kingdom upon earth, and according to the best calculation, is supposed to contain twenty-seven millions of inhabitants. From the reign of Sesostris to that of Boccharis, a term of near 800 years, but little is known of the princes who reigned, but it is believed from collateral evidence, that the country in that time continued in a very flourishing condition, and for aught that is known, enjoyed uninterrupted peace. Wars and commotions, (says an eminent writer,) are the greatest themes of the historian, while the gentle and happy reign of a wise prince passes unobserved and unrecorded. During this period of quietude at home, Egypt continued to pour forth her colonies into distant nations. Athens, that seat of learning and politeness, that school for all who aspired after wisdom, owes its foundation to Cecrops, who landed in Greece, with an Egyptian colony, before Christ 1585. The institutions which he established among the Athenians gave rise to the spread of the morals, arts and sciences in Greece, which have since shed their lustre upon Rome, Europe, and America.

From the reign of Boccharis to the dissolution of their government, the Egyptians are celebrated for the wisdom of their laws and political institutions, which were dictated by the true spirit of civil wisdom. It appears that this race of people, during their greatest prosperity, made but very little proficiency in the art of war. We hear of but little of their conquests of armies, which is an evidence of their being an unwarlike people.

On taking a slight view of the history of Europe, we find a striking contrast. Javan, the third from Noah, and son of Japhet, is the stock from whom all the people known by the name of Greeks are descended. Javan established himself in the islands on the Western coast of Asia Minor. It is supposed, and it may not be impossible, that a few wanderers would escape over into Europe. Who would believe, says a writer, that the Greeks, who in latter ages became the patterns of politeness and every elegant art, were descended from a savage race of men, traversing the woods and wilds, inhabiting the rocks and caverns, a wretched prey to wild beasts and to one another. I would here remark that it is a little singular that modern philosophers, the descendants of this race of savages, should claim for their race a superiority of intellect over those who, at that very time, were enjoying all the real benefits of civilized life.

The remnant of this race which found their way to Europe from Asia Minor, are brought into notice but very little until after Rome had conquered the world. On the decline of that empire, from the death of Theodosius the great, A. D. 395 to A. D. 571, all Europe exhibited a picture of most melancholy Gothic barbarity. Literature, science, taste, were words scarce in use from this period to the sixteenth century. Persons of the highest rank could not read or write. Many of the clergy did not understand the learning which they were obliged daily to write; some of them could scarce read it.

The Goths and Vandals, and other fierce tribes, who were scattered over the vast countries of the North of Europe and Northwest of Asia, were drawn from their homes by a thirst for blood and plunder. Great bodies of armed men, with their wives and children, issued forth like regular colonies in quest of new settlements. New adventurers followed them. The lands which they deserted were occupied by more remote tribes of barbarians. These in their turn, pushed into more fertile countries, and like a torrent continually increasing, rolled on, and swept every thing before them.

Wherever the barbarians marched, their route was marked with blood. They ravaged or destroyed all around them. They made no distinction between what was sacred and what was profane. They respected no age, or sex, or rank. If man was called upon, (says an eminent historian,) to fix upon the period in the history of the world, during which the condition of the human race was most calamitious and afflicted, he would, without hesitation, name that which elapsed from A. D. 395 to 511. Cotemporary authors, who beheld that scene of destruction, labor and are at a loss for expressions to describe the horror of it. The scourge of God, the destroyer of nations, are the dreadful epithets by which they distinguish the most noted of the barbarous leaders.

Towards the close of the sixth century, the Saxons or Germans were masters of the Southern and more fertile provinces of Britain: the Franks, another tribe of Germans; the Goths of Spain; the Goths and Lombards of Italy, and the adjacent provinces.

During the period above mentioned, European slavery was introduced. Having, as yet, the art of navigation but very imperfectly, it seemed to be the whole bent of their mind to enslave each other.

A form of government, distinguished by the name of the Feudal system, was one under which the leaders of these barbarians became intolerable. They reduced the great body of them to actual servitude. They were slaves fixed to the soil, and with it transferred from one proprietor to another, by sale, or by conveyance. The kindred and dependants of an aggressor, as well as of a defender, were involved in a quarrel, without even the liberty of remaining neuter, whenever their superiors saw fit.

The king or general to whom they belonged, would lead them on to conquest, parcel out the land of the vanquished among his chief officers, binding those on whom they were bestowed, to follow his standard with a number of men, and to bear arms in his defence. The chief officers imitated the example of their sovereign, and in distributing portions of their lands among their dependents, annexed the same conditions to the grant.

For the smallest pretext they would make war with one another, and lead their slaves on to conquest; and take the land and goods of their foes as the reward of their enterprise. This system existed in the highlands in Scotland, as late as the year 1156.

It is not a little remarkable, that in the nineteenth century a remnant of this same barbarous people should boast of their national superiority of intellect, and of wisdom and religion; who, in the seventeenth century, crossed the Atlantic and practised the same crime their barbarous ancestry had done in the fourth, fifth and sixth centuries: bringing with them the same boasted spirit of enterprise; and not unlike their fathers, staining their route with blood, as they have rolled along, as a cloud of locusts, towards the West. The late unholy war with the Indians, and the wicked crusade against the peace of Mexico, are striking illustrations of the nobleness of this race ot people, and the powers of their mind. I will here take a brief review of the events following each race from their beginning.

Before Christ 2188, Misraim, the son of Ham, founded the kingdom of Egypt, which lasted 1633 years.

2059, Ninus, the son of Belus, another branch of Ham's family, founds the kingdom of Assyria, which lasted 1000 years, and out of its ruins Babylon, Ninevah, and the kingdom of the Medes.

1822, Memnon, the Egyptian, invents the letters.

1571, Moses born in Egypt, and adopted by Pharaoh's daughter, who educated him in all the learning of the Egpytians.

1556, Cecrops brings a colony from Egypt into Attica, and begins the kingdom of Athens, in Greece.

1485, The first ship that appeared in Greece was brought from Egypt by Danaus, who arrived at Rhodes, and brought with him his fifty daughters.

869, The city of Carthage, in Africa, founded by queen Dido.

604, By order of Necho, king of Egypt, some Phenicians, sailed from the Red Sea round Africa, and returned by the Mediterranean.

600, Thales, of Miletus, travels to Egypt, to acquire the knowledge of geometry, astronomy, and philosophy; returns to Greece and calculates eclipses, gives general notions of the universe, &c.

285, Dionysius, of Alexandria, began his astronomical era, on Monday, June 26, being the first who found the exact solar year to consist of 365 days, 5 hours, and 49 minutes.

284, Ptolemy Philadelphus, king of Egypt, employs seventy-two interpreters to translate the Old Testament into the Greek language, which was called the Septuagint.

237, Hamilcar, the Carthagenian, causes his son Hannibal, at nine years of age, to swear eternal enmity to the Romans.

218, Hannibal passes the Alps, at the age of 28 years, and defeats the Romans in several battles.

47, The Alexandrian library, consisting of 400,000 valuable books burned by accident.

30, Alexandria is taken by Octavius, upon which Mark Antony and Cleopatra, put themselves to death, and Egypt is reduced to a Roman province.

640, A. D., Alexandria is taken by the Saracens, or followers of Mahomet, and the grand library burned by order of Omar, their caliph or prince.

991, The figures in arithmetic are brought into Europe by the Saracens from Arabia. [Poor negroes, I wonder where they got learning. These are the race of people who are charged with an inferiority of intellect.]

Africa could once boast of several states of eminence, among which are Egypt, Ethiopia, and Carthage; the latter supported an extensive commerce, which was extended to every part of the then known world. Her fleets even visited the British shores, and was every where prosperous, until she was visited with the scourge of war, which opened the way for those nations whose life depended on plunder. The Romans have the honor, by the assistance of the Mauritonians, of subduing Carthage; after which the North of Africa was overrun by the Vandals, who, in their march destroyed all arts and sciences; and, to add to the calamity of this quarter of the world, the Saracens made a sudden conquest of all the coasts of Egypt and Barbary, in the seventh century. And these were succeeded by the Turks, both being of the Mahomedan religion, whose professors carried desolation wherever they went; and thus the ruin of that once flourishing part of the world was completed. Since that period, Africa has been robbed of her riches and honor, and sons and daughters, to glut the rapacity of the great minds of European bigots.

The following is a short chronological view of the events following the rise of the Europeans.

A. D. 49, London is founded by the Romans.

51, Caractacus, the British king is carried in chains to Rome.

59, Nero persecutes the Druids in Britain.

61, The British queen defeats the Romans, but is conquered soon after by Suetonius, governor of Britain.

63, Christianity introduced into Britain.

85, Julius Agricola, governor of South Britain, to protect the civilized Britons from the incursions of the Caledonians, builds a line of forts between the rivers Forth and Clyde; defeats the Caledonians; and first sails round Britain, which he discovers to be an island.

222, About this time the barbarians begin their eruptions and the Goths have annual tribute not to molest the Roman government.

274, The art of manufacturing silk first introduced into Britain from India; the manufacturing of it introduced into Europe by some monks, 551.

404, The kingdom of Caledonia, or Scotland, revives under Fergus.

406, The Vandals, Alans, and Suevi spread in France and Spain, by a concession of Honorius, emperor of the West.

410, Rome taken and plundered by Alaric, king of visi-Goths.

412, The Vandals begin their kingdom in Spain.

446, The Romans having left the Britons to themselves, are greatly harassed by the Scots and Picts, they make their complaints to Rome again, which they entitle, the groans of the Britons.

449, The Saxons join the Britons against the Scots and Picts.

455, Saxons having repulsed the Scots and Picts begin to establish themselves in Kent under Hengist.

476, Several new states arise in Italy and other parts, consisting of Goths, Vandals, Huns, and other barbarians, under whom literature is extinguished, and the works of the learned are destroyed.

496, Clovis, king of France, baptized, and christianity begins in that kingdom.

508, Prince Arthur begins his reign over the Britons.

609, Here begins the power of the Pope by the concession of Phocas, emperor of the east.

685, The Britons, after a struggle of near 150 years, are totally expelled by the Saxons, and drove into Wales and Cornwall.

712, The Saracens conquer Spain.

726, The controversy about images occasions many insurrections.

800, Charlemagne, king of France, begins the empire of Germany, and endeavors to restore learning.

838, The Scots and Picts have a hard fight. The former prevail.

867, The Danes begin their ravages in England.

896, Alfred the Great fought 56 battles with the invading

Danes, after which he divides his kingdom into counties, hundreds, tythings; erects courts: and founds the University of Oxford.

936, The Saracen empire is divided into seven kingdoms, by usurpation.

1015, Children forbidden by law to be sold by their parents, in England.

1017, Canute, king of Denmark, gets possession of England.

1040, The Danes after much hard fighting are driven out of Scotland.

1041, The Saxon line restored under Edward.

1043, The Turks who had hitherto fought for other nations, have become formidable, and take possession of Persia.

1059, Malcolm III. king of Scotland, kills Macbeth, and marries the princess Margaret.

1065, The Turks take Jerusalem.

1066, The conquest of England by William; who

1070, introduced the feudal law.

1075, Henry IV, emperor of Germany, and the Pope, have a quarrel. Henry, in penance walks barefoot in January.

1096, The first crusade to the Holy Land is begun, under several Christian princes, to drive the infidels from Jerusalem.

1118, The order of knight templars instituted.

1172, Henry II, king of England, takes possession of Ireland.

1182, Pope Alexander III, compels the kings of France and England, to hold the stirrups of his saddle when he mounted his horse.

1192, Richard, king of England, defeats Saladin's army, consisting of 300,000 combatants.

1200, Chimnies not known in England.

1227, The Tartars emerge from the Northern part of Asia, and in imitation of former conquerers, carry death and desolation wherever they march. They overrun all the Saracen empire.

1233, The inquisition began in 1204, is now in the hands of the Dominicans.

1258, The Tartars take Bagdad, which finishes the empire of the Saracens.

1263, Acho, king of Norway, invades Scotland with 160 sail, and lands 20,000 men at the mouth of the Clyde, who were cut to pieces by Alexander III.

1273, The empire of the present Austrian family begins in Germany.

1282, Lewellyn, prince of Wales, defeated and killed by Edward I., who unites that principality to England.

1314, Battle between Edward II, and Robert Bruce, which establishes the latter on the throne of Scotland.

1340, Gunpowder and guns first invented by Swartz. 1346, Bombs and four pieces of cannon were made, by which Edward III. gained the battle of Cressy.

1346, The battle of Durham, in which David, king of Scots, is taken prisoner.

1356, The battle of Poictiers, in which king John of France and his son are taken prisoners by Edward, the black prince.

1362, John Wickliffe calls in question the doctrines of the church of Rome, whose followers are called Lollards.

1388, The battle of Otterburn between Hotspur and the Earl of Douglas.

1415, Battle gained over the French by Henry V. of England.

1428, The siege of Orleans.

1453, Constantinople taken by the Turks.

1483, Civil war ended between the house of York and Lancaster, after a siege of 30 years, and the loss of 100,000 men.

1489, Maps and sea charts first brought to England.

1492, America first discovered by Columbus.

1494, Algebra first known in Europe.

1497, South America first discovered.

1499, North America by Cabot.

1517, Martin Luther begins the reformation.

1616, The first permanent settlement in Virginia.

1621, New England planted by the Puritans.

1635, Province of Maryland planted by Lord Baltimore.

1640, The massacre in Ireland, when 40,000 English protestants are killed.

1649, Charles I. beheaded.

3

1664, The New Netherlands in North America, taken from the Swedes and Dutch by the English.

1667, The peace of Breda, which confirms to the English the New Netherlands, now known by names of Pennsylvania, New York, and New Jersey.

The object I have in introducing this account of events, attendant on the rise and progress of the African and European nations, is, that the traits of their national character may at a glance be discovered; by which the reader may the better judge of the superiority of the descendants of Japhet over those of Ham. In the first place, the European branch of Japhet's family have but very little claims to the rank of civilized nations. From the fourth up to the sixteenth century, they were in the deepest state of heathenish barbarity. A continual scene of bloodshed and robbery was attendant on the increase of their numbers. Their spread over different countries caused almost an entire extinction of all civil and religious governments, and of the liberal arts and sciences. And even since that period, all Europe and America have been little else than one great universal battle field.

It is true, there is a great advance in the arts and sciences from where they once were; but whether they are any where near its standard, as they once existed in Africa, is a matter of strong doubt. We should without doubt, had not the Europeans destroyed every vestige of history, which fell in their barbarous march, been favored with an extensive and minute history of the now unknown parts of Africa. Certain it is, however, that whatever they may have contributed of knowledge to the world, it is owing to these casual circumstances we have mentioned, rather than any thing peculiar to them as a people.

Any one who has the least conception of true greatness, on comparing the two races by means of what history we have, must decide in favor of the descendants of Ham. The Egyptians alone have done more to cultivate such improvements as comports to the happiness of mankind, than all the descendants of Japhet put together. Their enterprise in establishing colonies and governments among their barbarous neighbors, and supplying their wants from their granaries, instead of taking the advantage of their ignorance, and robbing them of what little they had, does not look much like an inferiority of intellect, nor a want of disposition to make a proper use of it. They, at no age, cultivated the art of war to any great extent. Neither are they found making an aggressive war with any nation. But, while other nations were continually robbing and destroying each other, they were cultivating internal improvement; and virtually became a storehouse of every thing conducive to the happiness of mankind, with which she supplied their wants. Even as late as Carthage was in her glory, that race of people exhibited their original character. For that famed city never acquired its greatness, but by the cultivation of commerce. And though she obtained command of both sides of the Mediterranean, became mistress of the sea, made the islands of Corsica and Sardinia tributary to her, yet it is evident she acquired this advantage by her wealth, rather than by her arms.

Europe and America presents quite a different spectacle. There is not a foot of God's earth which is now occupied by them, but has been obtained, in effect, by the dint of war, and the destruction of the vanquished, since the founding of London, A. D. 49. Their whole career presents a motley mixture of barbarism and civilization, of fraud and philanthropy, of patriotism and avarice, of religion and bloodshed. And notwithstanding many great and good men have lived and died bright luminaries of the world—and notwithstanding there are many now living who are the seed of the church, yet it must be admitted that almost every nation in Europe, and especially Americans, retain, in principle, if not in manners, all the characteristics of their barbarous and avaricious ancestors. And instead of their advanced state in science being attributable to a superior developement of intellectual faculties, there is nothing more capable of proof, than that it is solely owing to the nature of the circumstances into which they were drawn by their innate thirst for blood and plunder.

Had the inhabitants of Egypt, Ethiopia, Carthage, and other

kingdoms in Africa, been possessed with the same disposition, the probability is, that the world now would be in a heathenish darkness, for the want of that information which their better disposition has been capable of producing. And had they had the means at that early age of understanding human nature, as they now would have, were their kingdoms in their glory, they would probably not have suffered their liberality to be taken advantage of by a barbarous crew around them. It is not for the want of mind, therefore, that Africa is in her present state; for were the dispositions of her different nations like the ancient barbarians of Europe, they would soon make a plenty of business for Europeans, with all their advantages, to defend themselves against their depredations. But it is not the genius of the race. Nothing but liberal, generous principles, can call the energies of an African mind into action. And when these principles are overruled by a foreign cause, they are left without any thing to inspire them to action, other than the cravings of their animal wants.

Africa never will raise herself, neither will she be raised by others, by warlike implements, or ardent spirits; nor yet by a hypocritical religious crusade, saying one thing and meaning another. But when she rises, other nations will have learned to deal justly with her from principle. When that time shall arrive, the lapse of a few generations will show the world that her sons will again take the lead in the field of virtuous enterprise, filling the front ranks of the church, when she marches into the millennial era.

CHAPTER I.

ON THE INTELLECTUAL CHARACTER OF THE COLORED PEOPLE
OF THESE UNITED STATES OF AMERICA.

In this country we behold the remnant of a once noble, but
now heathenish people. In calling the attention of my readers
to the subject which I here present them, I would have them
lose sight of the African character, about which I have made
some remarks in my introduction. For at this time, circumstances have established as much difference between them and their
ancestry, as exists between them and any other race or nation.
In the first place the colored people who are born in this country, are Americans in every sense of the word. Americans by
birth, genius. habits, language, &c. It is supposed, and I think
not without foundation, that the slave population labor under
an intellectual and physical disability or inferiority. The
justness of these conclusions, however, will apply only to such
as have been subject to slavery some considerable length of
time.

I have already made some remarks with regard to the cause
of apparent differences between nations. I shall have cause to
remark again, that as the intellectual as well as the physical
properties of mankind, are subject to cultivation, I have observed that the growth or culture depends materially on the
means employed to that end. In those countries in which the
maxims and laws are such as are calculated to employ the physical properties mostly, such as racing, hunting, &c., there is
uniformly a full development of physical properties. We will
take the American Indian for example. A habit of indolence
produces a contrary effect. History, as well as experience, will
justify me in saying that a proper degree of exercise is essential to the growth of the corporeal system ; and that the form
and size depends on the extent and amount of exercise. On

comparing one who is brought up from his youth a trades-
man, with one who is brought up a farmer, the difference is
manifestly apparent according to the difference of their exercise.
Change of public sentiment indirectly affects the form and size of
whole nations, inasmuch as public sentiment dictates the mode
and kind of exercise. The muscular yeomanry who once formed
a majority of our country's population, are now but seldom
found ; those who fill their places in society, in no way compare with them in that respect. Compare our farmer's daughters, who have been brought up under the influence of country
habits, with those brought up under city habits, and a difference
is most manifest.

But there is another consideration worthy of notice. Education, says D. D. Hunter,* on the part of the mother, commences from the moment she has the prospect of being a mother.
And her own health thenceforth is the first duty she owes to
her child. The instructions given to the wife of Manoah, and
mother of Sampson, the Nazarite, (Jud. 13, 4 :) 'Now, therefore,
beware, I pray thee, drink not wine nor strong drink, and eat
not any unclean thing,' are not merely arbitrarily adapted only
to a particular branch of political economy, and intended to
serve local and temporary purposes ; no, the constitutions of
nature, reason, and experience, which unite in recommending
to those who have the prospect of being mothers, a strict attention to diet, to exercise, to temper, to every thing, which affecting
the frame of their own body or mind, may communicate an important, a lasting, perhaps indelible impression, to the mind or
body of their offspring. A proper regimen for themselves, is
therefore the first stage of education for their children. The
neglect of it is frequently found productive of effects which no
future culture is able to alter or rectify.

These most just remarks confirm me in the opinion, that the
laws of nature may be crossed by the misconduct or misfortune
of her who has the prospect of being a mother. Apply these
remarks to the condition of slave mothers, as such, and what are
the plain and natural inferences to be drawn. Certainly, if they
are entitled to any weight at all, the intellectual and physical
inferiority of the slave population can be accounted for without
imputing it to an original hereditary cause. Contemplate the
exposed condition of slave mothers—their continual subjection
to despotism and barbarity ; their minds proscribed to the narrow bounds of servile obedience, subject to irritation from every

* Hunter's Sacred Biography, vol. 7. page 10.

quarter; great disappointment, and physical suffering themselves, and continual eye-witnesses to maiming and flagellation; shrieks of wo borne to their ears on every wind. Indeed, language is lame in the attempt to describe the condition of those poor daughters of affliction. Indeed, I have no disposition to dwell on the subject; to be obliged to think of it at all, is sufficiently harrowing to my feelings. But I would inquire how it can be possible for nature, under such circumstances, to act up to her perfect laws?

The approbrious terms used in common by most all classes, to describe the deformities of the offspring of these parents, is true in part, though employed with rather bad grace by those in whom the cause of their deformity originates. I will introduce those terms, not for the sake of embellishing my treatise with their modest style, but to show the lineal effects of slavery on its victims. Contracted and sloped foreheads; prominent eye-balls; projecting under-jaw; certain distended muscles about the mouth, or lower parts of the face; thick lips and flat nose; hips and rump projecting; crooked shins; flat feet, with large projecting heels. This, in part, is the language used by moderns to philosophize, upon the negro character. With regard to their mind, it is said that their intellectual brain is not fully developed; malicious disposition; no taste for high and honorable attainments; implacable enemies one to another; and that they sustain the same relation to the ourang outang, that the whites do to them.

Now, as it respects myself, I am perfectly willing to admit the truth of these remarks, as they apply to the character of a slave population; for I am aware that no language capable of being employed by mortal tongue, is sufficiently descriptive to set forth in its true character the effect of that cursed thing, slavery. I shall here be under the necessity of calling up those considerations connected with the subject, which I but a little time since entertained a hope that I should be able to pass by unnoticed; I have reference to a mother who is a slave, bringing into the world beings whose limbs and minds were lineally fashioned for the yoke and fetter, long before her own immortal mind was clothed in materiality.

I would ask my readers to think of woman as the greatest natural gift to man—think of her in delicate health, when the poor delicate fabric is taxed to the utmost to answer the demands of nature's laws—when friends and sympathies, nutricious aliments, and every other collateral aid is needed. O think of poor woman, a prospective mother; and when you think, feel as a heart of flesh can feel; see her weeping eyes fixed alternately upon the object of her affections and him who accounts her a brute—think how she feels on beholding the gore streaming from the back, the naked back, of the former, while the latter wields the accursed lash, until the back of a husband, indeed the whole frame, has become like a loathsome heap of mangled flesh. How often has she witnessed the wielding club lay him prostrate, while the purple current followed the damning blow. How the rattling of the chain, the lock of which has worn his ancles and his wrists to the bone, falls upon her ear. O, has man fallen so far below the dignity of his original character, as not to be susceptible of feeling. But does the story stop here. I would that it were even so. But alas! this, the ornamental production of nature's God, is not exempt, even in this state, from the task of a slave. And, as though cursed by all the gods, her own delicate frame is destined to feel the cruel scourge. When faint and weary she lags her step, the overseer, as though decreed to be a tormenting devil, throws the coiling lash upon her naked back; and in turn, the master makes it his pleasure to despoil the works of God, by subjecting her to the rank of goods and chattels, to be sold in the shambles. Woman, you who possess a woman's nature, can feel for her who was destined by the Creator of you both, to fill the same sphere with yourself. You know by experience the claims of nature's laws—you know too well the irritability of your natures when taxed to the utmost to fulfil the decree of nature's God.

I have in part given a description of a mother that is a slave. And can it be believed to be possible for such a one to bring perfect children into the world. If we are permitted to decide that natural causes produce natural effects, then it must be equally true that unnatural causes produce unnatural effects. The slave system is an unnatural cause, and has produced its unnatural effects, as displayed in the deformity of two and a half millions of beings, who have been under its soul-and-body-destroying influence, lineally, for near three hundred years; together with all those who have died their progenitors since that period.

But again, I believe it to be an axiom generally admitted, that mind acts on matter, then again, that mind acts on mind; this being the case, is it a matter of surprise that those mothers who are slaves, should, on witnessing the distended muscles on the face of whipped slaves, produce the same or similar distensions on the face of her offspring, by her own mind being affected by the sight; and so with all other deformities. Like causes produce like effects. If by Jacob's placing ring-streaked elder in the trough where Laban's flocks drank, caused their young to be ring-streaked and speckled, why should not the offspring of slave mothers, who are continually witnessing exciting objects, be affected by the same law; and why should they not be more affected, as the mother is capable of being more excited.

From the foregoing I draw the following conclusions, with regard to the different degrees of effect produced by slavery. Compare slaves that are African born, with those who are born in slavery, and the latter will in no wise compare with the former in point of form of person or strength of mind. The first and second generation born in this country are generally far before the fourth and fifth, in this respect. Compare such as have been house servants, as they are called, for several generations with such as have been confined to plantations the same term of time, and there will be a manifest inferiority in the latter. Observe among the nominally free, their form of person, features, strength of mind, and bent of genius, fidelity, &c., and it will evidently appear that they who sustain a relation of no further than the third generation from African birth, are in general far before those who sustain a more distant relation. The former generally acquire small possessions, and conform their habits of life and modes of operation with those common where they live, while those who have been enslaved for several generations, or whose progenitors in direct line were thus enslaved, cannot be induced to conform to any regular rule of life or operation. I intend this last statement as general fact, of which, however, there are exceptions; where there is a mixture of blood, as it is sometimes called, perhaps these remarks may not apply. I suppose, however, that in case of a union between a degraded American slave of the last order spoken of, and a highly intelligent free American, whether white or colored, that the offspring of such parents are as likely to partake of the influence of slavery through the lineal medium of the slave parent, as to receive natural intelligence through the medium of the other.

So far as I understand, nature's law seems not to be scrupulously rigid in this particular: there appears to be no rule, therefore, by which to determine the effect or lineal influence of slavery on a mixed race. I am satisfied with regard to one fact, however, that caste has no influence whatever: for a union between a highly cultivated black and a degraded one, produces an exact similar effect. Whatever complexion or nation parents thus connected

4

may be of, the effect produced would be the same, but it would not be certain that their children would occupy a midway region between the intelligent and degraded parent, as in other cases part of a family may be below mediocrity, and part above, in point of form and intellect. One thing is certain, which may have some bearing in the case ; that when nature has been robbed, give her a fair chance and she will repair her loss by her own operations, one of which is to produce variety. But to proceed further with any remarks on this point, I feel myself not at liberty. In view of what I have said on this subject, I am aware of having fallen short of giving a full description of the lineal influence and effects slavery has upon the colored population of this country. Such is the nature of the subject, that it is almost impossible to arrange our thoughts so as to follow it by any correct rule of investigation.

Slavery, in its effects, is like that of a complicated disease, typifying evil in all its variety—in its operations, omnipotent to destroy—in effect, fatal as death and hell. Language is·lame in its most successful attempt, to describe its enormity ; and with all the excitement which this country has undergone, in consequence of the discussion of the subject, yet the story is not half told, neither can it be. We, who are subject to its fatal effects, cannot fully realize the disease under which we labor. Think of a colored community, whose genius and temperament of minds all differ in proportion as they are lineally or personally made to feel the damning influence of slavery, and, as though it had the gift of creating tormenting pangs at pleasure, it comes up, in the character of an accuser, and charges our half destroyed, discordant minds, with hatred one towards the other, as though a body composed of parts, and systematized by the laws of nature, were capable of continuing its regular configurative movements after it has been decomposed.

When I think of nature's laws, that with scrupulous exactness they are to be obeyed by all things over which they are intended to bear rule, in order that she may be able to declare, in all her variety, that the hand that made her is divine, and when, in this case, I see and feel how she has been robbed of her means to perform her delightful task—her laws trampled under feet with all their divine authority, despoiling her works even in her most sacred temples—I wonder that I am a man ; for though of the third generation from slave parents, yet in body and mind nature has never been permitted to half finish her work. Let all judge who is in the fault, God, or slavery, or its sustainers?

CHAPTER II.

ON THE POLITICAL CONDITION AND CHARACTER OF THE COLORED PEOPLE.

A government like this is at any time liable to be revolutionized by the people, at any and every time there is a change of public sentiment. This, perhaps, is as it should be. But when the subjects of a republican government become morally and politically corrupt, there is but little chance remaining for republicanism. A correct standard may be set up, under which parties may pretend to aim at a defence of the original principles upon which the government was based ; but if the whole country has become corrupt, what executive power is there remaining to call those parties in question, and to decide whether their pretensions and acts correspond with the standard under which they profess to act. Suppose the Constitution and articles of confederation, be the admitted correct standard by all parties, still the case is no better, when there is not honesty enough in either, to admit a fair construction of their letter and spirit. Good laws, and a good form of government, are of but very little use to a wicked people, further than they are able to restrain them from wickedness.

Were a fallen angel permitted to live under the government of heaven, his disposition would first incline him to explain away the nature of its laws ; this done, their spirit becomes perverted, which places him back in hell from whence he came ; for, though he could not alter the laws of heaven, yet he could pervert their use, in himself, and act them out in this perverted state, which would make him act just like a devil. The perversion of infinite good, is infinite evil—and if the spiritual use of the laws of an infinitely perfect government is productive of a perfect heaven, in like manner their spiritual perversion is productive of perfect or infinite hell. Hence it is said to be a bottomless pit—ay, deep as the principle is high, from which the distortion is made.

I have taken this course to illustrate the state of a people with a good government and laws, and with a disposition to explain away all their meaning. My conclusions are, that such republicans are capable, like the angel about which I have spoken, to carry out their republicanism into the most fatal despotism. A republican form of government, therefore, can be a blessing to no people, further than they make honest virtue the rule of life. Indeed, honesty is essential to the existence of a republican form of government, for it originates in a contract or agreement of its subjects, relative to the disposal of their mutual interests. If conspiracy is got up by any of the contracters, against the fundamental principles of the honest contract, (which, if republican, embraced those interests which are unalienable, and no more,) and if, by an influence gained by them, so as to make its intent null and void, the foundation of the government is thereby destroyed; leaving its whole fabric a mere wreck, inefficient in all its executive power. Or if the contract had the form of honesty only, when there was a secret design of fraud in the minds of the parties contracting, then of course, it is a body without a soul—a fabric without a foundation; and, like a dead carcass entombed, will tumble to pieces as soon as brought to the light of truth, and into the pure air of honesty.

With regard to the claims of the colored subjects of this government to equal political rights, I maintain that their claims are founded in an original agreement of the contracting parties, and that there is nothing to show that color was a consideration in the agreement. It is well known that when the country belonged to Great Britain, the colored people were slaves. But when America revolted from Britain, they were held no longer by any legal power. There was no efficient law in the land except marshal law, and that regarded no one as a slave. The inhabitants were governed by no other law, except by resolutions adopted from time to time by meetings convoked in the different colonies. Upon the face of the warrants by which these district and town meetings were called, there is not a word said about the color of the attendants. In convoking the continental Congress of the 4th of September, 1776, there was not a word said about color. In November of the same year, Congress met again, to get in readiness twelve thousand men to act in any emergency; at the same time, a request was forwarded to Connecticut, New Hampshire, and Rhode Island, to increase this army to twenty thousand men. Now it is well known that hun-

dreds of the men of which this army was composed, were colored men, and recognized by Congress as Americans.

An extract from the speech of Richard Henry Lee, delivered
in Congress, assembled June 8, 1776, in support of a motion,
which he offered, to declare America free and independent, will
give some view of the nature of the agreement upon which this
government is based. ' The eyes of all Europe are fixed upon
us ; she demands of us a living example of freedom, that may
contrast, by the felicity of her citizens, (I suppose black as
well as white,) with the ever increasing tyranny which desolates
her polluted shores. She invites us to prepare an asylum where
the unhappy may find solace, and the persecuted, repose. She
entreats us to cultivate a propitious soil, where that generous
plant which first sprang up and grew in England, but is now
withered by the poisonous blasts of Scottish tyranny, may revive
and flourish, sheltering under its salubrious and interminable
shade all the unfortunate of the human race.'

The principles which this speech contains, are manifestly
those which were then acted upon. To remove all doubt
on this point, I will make a short extract from the Declaration of Independence, in Congress assembled, fourth of
July, 1776. ' We, the representatives of these United States
of America, in general Congress assembled, appealing to
the Supreme Judge of the world for the rectitude of our
intentions, and by the authority of the good people of these
Colonies, solemnly publish and declare, that these united colonies are, and of right ought to be, free and independent States.
(And now for the pledge.) We mutually pledge to each other
our lives, our fortunes, and our sacred honor.' The representatives who composed that Congress were fifty-five in number, and
all signed the declaration and pledge in behalf of the good people of the thirteen States.

Now I would ask, can it be said, from any fair construction of
the foregoing extracts, that the colored people are not recognized as citizens. Congress drew up articles of confederation also,
among which are found the following reserved state privileges.
' Each state has the exclusive right of regulating its internal
government, and of framing its own laws, in all matters not included in the articles of confederation, and which are not repugnant to it.' Another article reads as follows : ' There shall be
a public treasury for the service of the confederation, to be re-
plenished by the particular contributions of each state, the same
to be proportioned according to the number of inhabitants of
every age, sex, or condition, with the exception of Indians.'

These extracts are sufficient to show the civil and political recognition of the colored people. In addition to which, however, we have an official acknowledgment of their equal, civil, and political relation to the government, in the following proclamation of Major General Andrew Jackson, to the colored people of Louisiana, Sept. 21, 1814 ; also of Thomas Butler, Aid de Camp :

'*Head Quarters, Seventh Military District, Mobile, September* 21, 1814. *To the Free Colored Inhabitants of Louisiana.*

'Through a mistaken policy you have heretofore been deprived of a participation in the glorious struggle for national rights, in which our country is engaged. This no longer shall exist.

' As sons of Freedom, you are now called upon to defend our most inestimable blessing. As Americans, your country looks with confidence to her adopted children, for a valorous support, as a faithful return for the advantages enjoyed under her mild and equitable government. As fathers, husbands, and brothers, you are summoned to rally round the standard of the Eagle, to defend all which is dear in existence.

' Your country, although calling for your exertions, does not wish you to engage in her cause, without remunerating you for the services rendered. Your intelligent minds are not to be led away by false representations—your love of honor would cause you to despise the man who should attempt to deceive you. In the sincerity of a soldier, and the language of truth, I address you.

' To every noble hearted free man of color, volunteering to serve during the present contest with Great Britain and no longer, there will be paid the same bounty in money and lands, now received by the white soldiers of the United States, viz., one hundred and twenty-four dollars in money, and one hundred and sixty acres of land. The non-commissioned officers and privates will also be entitled to the same monthly pay and daily rations and clothes, furnished to any American soldier.

' On enrolling yourselves in companies, the Major General commanding, will select officers for your government, from your white fellow citizens. Your non-commissioned officers will be appointed from among yourselves.

' Due regard will be paid to the feelings of freemen and soldiers. You will not, by being associated with white men in the same corps, be exposed to improper comparisons or unjust sarcasm. As a distinct, independent battalion or regiment, pursu-ing the path of glory, you will, undivided, receive the applause and gratitude of your countrymen.

' To assure you of the sincerity of my intentions, and my anxiety to engage your invaluable services to our country, I have communicated my wishes to the Governor of Louisiana, who is fully informed as to the manner of enrolments, and will give you every necessary information on the subject of this address.

' ANDREW JACKSON, *Major General Commmanding.*'

' *Proclamation to the Free People of Color.*

' Soldiers!—When on the banks of the Moble, I called you to take arms, inviting you to partake the perils and glory of your white fellow citizens, *I expected much from you;* for I was not ignorant that you possessed qualities most formidable to an invading enemy. I knew with what fortitude you could endure hunger and thirst, and all the fatigues of a campaign. *I knew well how you loved your native country*, and that you had, as well as ourselves, to defend what man holds most dear— his parents, relations, wife, children and property: *You have done more than I expected.* In addition to the previous quali-ties I before knew you to possess, I found moreover, among you, a noble enthusiasm which leads to the performance of great things.

' Soldiers!—The President of the United States shall hear how praiseworthy was your conduct in the hour of danger, and the representatives of the American people will, I doubt not, give you the praise your exploits entitle you to. Your General an-ticipates them in applauding your noble ardor.

' The enemy approaches, his vessels cover our lakes ; our brave citizens are united, and all contention has ceased among them. Their only dispute is, who shall win the prize of valor, or who the most glory, its noblest reward.

' By Order, THOMAS BUTLER, *Aid de Camp.*'

All the civil and political disabilities of the colored people, are the effect of usurpation. It is true, slavery is recognized by the articles of confederation ; but there is not a public docu-ment of the government, which recognizes a colored man as a slave, not even in the provision for Southern representation.

When fugitive slaves are demanded by Southern slaveholders, they are recovered by virtue of a provision made to recover prisoners held to labor, in the state from whence they have ab-sconded ; but how that provision can be construed in such a manner, as to give them that advantage, I cannot conceive. I am satisfied, that it only serves as a pretext to justify a base perversion of the law, for the sake of pleasing evil doers. In the first place, a slave is not held to labor legally in slave states, because, according to the extract I have made, viz., that each state has a right to frame laws which are not *prejudicial* to the articles of confederation ; there is a limitation to which every other article of the document is subject. Now, what says another article of confederation ? Why, that a person held to labor, shall be recovered. But in what way held ? Upon this the articles of confederation, are silent ; in fact, they may as well be silent ; for had they pointed out the manner of persons being held to labor, they would have assumed the province of common law ; this, the framers of the constitution and documents of confederation, knew full well ; and the administrators of justice now know, that no person under heaven can be held to labor, other than by virtue of a contract, recognizable by common law. Neither do the administrators of justice, found their decisions on any thing found in the articles of confederation ; for a proof of which, I will call the attention of my readers to the following considerations.

If a white person is arraigned before a justice, as a fugitive slave, it would not be all the evidence that could be collected to prove him a slave, however true, that would induce a justice at the North to give him up, if he were able to prove that he was of white parentage. It would be the same, in case that an Indian was arraigned. There have been such claims made, I believe, and the defendants acquitted, even where there was proof positive, on the part of the claimant. This is proof positive, that decisions in such cases are not founded on a sentence contained in the articles of confederation, for there is nothing said, in that instrument, about nation or complexion ; but persons held to labor. Now, if it is by virtue of that instrument, that the black man is held to labor, why not hold the white person, and the Indian, by the same power ? And if they cannot be held by that instrument, how can any person be held, when no particular person is described ? It is evident that decisions in favor of claimants are founded in the fact of the defendants being a black person, or descendants of blacks or Africans. Now, for all this mode of administering justice, there cannot be found a single sentence of justification, in any public document in the country, except such as have been framed by individual states ; and these are prejudicial to the articles of confederation. If there is any thing in the articles of confederation, which justifies such a course of procedure, I have never found it. Only think, if one is claimed who is black, or who is a descendant of a black, (though he be whiter than a white man,) he must be given up to hopeless bondage, by virtue of the articles of confederation, when there is not a word about *black* contained in the instrument; whereas, if a white person be claimed, if he is half negro, if he can prove himself legally white, or of white parentage, he is acquitted. This course of conduct would be scouted by heathens, as a gross libel upon humanity and justice. It is so ; and a violation of the Constitution, and of the Bill of Rights—the rights of the people ; and every State which connives at such robbing in high places, clothed with a legal form, without a vestige of legal authority ; and that too, after having taken the tremendous *oath*, as recorded in the Declaration of Independence, ought to have *perjury* written upon their statute books, and upon the ceiling of their legislative halls, in letters as large as their crime, and as black as the complexion of the injured.

Excuses have been employed in vain to cover up the hypocrisy of this nation. The most corrupt policy which ever disgraced its barbarous ancestry, has been adopted by both church and state, for the avowed purpose of withholding the *inalienable rights* of one part of the subjects of the government. Pretexts of the lowest order, which are neither witty or decent, and which rank among that order of subterfuges, under which the lowest of ruffians attempt to hide, when exposed to detection, are made available. Indeed, I may say in candor, that a highwayman or assassin acts upon principles far superior, in some respects, in comparison with those under which the administrators of the laws of church and state act, especially in their attempts to hide themselves and their designs from the just censure of the world, and from the burning rays of truth. I have no language to express what I see, and hear, and feel, on this subject. Were I capable of dipping my pen in the deepest dye of crime, and of understanding the science of the bottomless pit, I should then fail in presenting to the intelligence of mortals on earth, the true nature of American deception. There can be no appeals made in the name of the laws of the country, of philanthropy, or humanity, or religion, that is capable of drawing forth any thing but the retort,—*you are a negro!* If we call to our aid the thunder tones of the cannon and the arguments of fire arms, (vigorously managed by black and white men, side by side,) as displayed upon Dorchester Heights, and at Lexington, and at White Plains, and at Kingston, and at

5

Long Island, and elsewhere, the retort is, *you are a negro* —if we present to the nation a Bunker's Hill, our nation's altar, (upon which she offered her choicest sacrifice,) with our fathers, and brothers, and sons, prostrate thereon, wrapped in fire and smoke—the incense of blood borne upward upon the wings of sulphurous vapor, to the throne of national honor, with a halo of national glory echoing back, and spreading and astonishing the civilized world;—and if we present the thousands of widows and orphans, whose only earthly protectors were thus sacrificed, weeping over the fate of the departed; and anon, tears of blood are extorted, on learning that the government for which their lovers and sires had died, refuses to be their protector;—if we tell that angels weep in pity, and that God, the eternal Judge, ' will hear the desire of the humble, judge the fatherless and the oppressed, that the man of the earth may no more oppress,'—the retort is, YOU ARE A NEGRO! If there is a spark of honesty, patriotism, or religion, in the heart or the source from whence such refuting arguments emanate, the devil incarnate is the brightest seraph in paradise.

CHAPTER III.

ON THE NATURE OF THE PREJUDICE OF THE WHITE POPULA-
TION OF THE UNITED STATES, IN ITS MALIGNANT EXERCISE
TOWARDS THE COLORED PEOPLE.

Malignant prejudice is a principle which calls into action the
worst passions of the human heart. There are cases, however,
in which the exercise of prejudice is perfectly harmless. A
person may prepossess favorable opinions of another, and such
opinions may be just and right. Unfavorable opinions may be
formed, also, of persons whose conduct is censurable ; and a
just prejudice may be exercised towards them, as they stand
related to their own bad conduct, without a display of any
malignity.

Again, prejudicial feelings may be exercised towards another,
through an error of judgment, for the want of means of knowing the true character of those against whom a prejudice is in-
dulged ; in which case, it possesses nothing malignant, because
its possessor entertains no purpose of injury. Great caution
should be exercised, however, in judging the motives and conduct of another, especially when such conduct relates somewhat to ourselves—because it is very natural for us to be governed by our interest, or imaginary interest, which is liable to
lead us into errors of the worst kind. It is also natural, on
being convicted of wrong, to plead ignorance. But such a
plea will not always excuse the pleader in strict justice. For
if the prejudiced person has the means of knowing, or if he has
any doubt with regard to the justness of his opinions of his
neighbors, and still neglects to use the means of informing himself, and to solve his doubts on the subject, but persists in the
exercise of his prejudice, he is equally guilty of all the mischief
produced thereby, as he would be if he knew ever so well, and
persisted in his wrong course in the light of that knowledge.

Prejudice seems to possess a nature peculiar to itself It never possesses any vitiating qualities, except when it is exercised by one who has done, or intends to do, another an injury. And its malignity is heightened in proportion as its victim in any way recovers, or has a manifest prospect of recovering the injury ; or if there is apparently a door open by which a superior power to that which he possesses, may bring him to an account for the wrong done to his neighbor, all have a direct tendency to heighten the malignity of prejudice in the heart of its possessor.

The colored population are the injured party. And the prejudice of the whites against them is in exact proportion to the injury the colored people have sustained. There is a prejudice in this country against the Irish, who are flocking here by thousands. Still there is nothing malignant in the nature and exercise of that prejudice, either national or personal. It grows out of the mere circumstance of their different manners and religion. The moment an Irishman adopts the maxims and prevailing religion of the country, he is no longer regarded an Irishman, other than by birth. It is to be remembered, also, that the Irish are not an injured, but a benefited party ; therefore, it is not possible that the bestower of benefits could be at the same time malignantly exercising prejudice towards those he is benefiting.

There exists, therefore, no injurious prejudice against the Irish. There exists a prejudice against the Indians, but it is almost entirely national, and for the very reason that the injury they have sustained is essentially national. The jealous eye of this nation is fixed upon them as a nation, and has ever exercised the rigor of its prejudice towards them, in proportion as they attempted to recover their rightful possessions; or, in other words, just in proportion as the physical powers of the Indians, have dwindled to inefficiency, prejudice against them has become lax and passive. It revives only as they show signs of national life.

The injury sustained by the colored people, is both national and personal ; indeed, it is national in a twofold sense. In the first place, they are lineally stolen from their native country, and detained for centuries, in a strange land, as hewers of wood and drawers of water. In this situation, their blood, habits, minds, and bodies, have undergone such a change, as to cause them to lose all legal or natural relations to their mother country. They are no longer her children; therefore, they sustain the great injury of losing their country, their birthright, and are made aliens and illegitimates. Again, they sustain a national injury by being adopted subjects and citizens, and then be denied their citizenship, and the benefits derivable therefrom —accounted as aliens and outcasts, hence, are identified as belonging to no country—denied birthright in one, and had it stolen from them in another—and, I had like to have said, they had lost title to both worlds; for certainly they are denied all title in this, and almost all advantages to prepare for the next. In this light of the subject, they belong to no people, race, or nation ; subjects of no government—citizens of no country— scattered surplus remnants of two races, and of different nations—severed into individuality—rendered a mass of broken fragments, thrown to and fro, by the boisterous passions of this and other ungodly nations. Such, in part, are the national injuries sustained by this miserable people.

I am aware that most people suppose the existence of color to be the cause of malignant prejudice. Upon this supposition an argument is founded, that color is an insurmountable barrier, over which there can be no social or political relation formed between white and colored Americans. To show the folly of which, I shall lay down and sustain the following principles.

First. Effects, according to their numerous laws, partake of their parent cause in nature and quantity ; i. e. the amount of effect produced, will exactly agree with the amount of efficiency the cause contains which produced it ; and their legitimacy claims for them, the nature of their parent. Apply this rule to the subject under consideration, and it will be seen, that, if color were the cause of prejudice, it follows, that just according to the variegation of the cause, (color) so would the effect variegate— i. e. the clear blooded black would be subject to a greater degree of prejudice, in proportion as he was black—and those of lighter caste subject to a less degree of prejudice, as they were light. Now it is well known that the exercise of prejudice, is as intense towards those who are in fact whiter than a clear blooded American, as it is against one who is as black as jet, if they are identified as belonging to that race of people who are the injured party.

Again. That which cannot be contemplated as a principle, abstractly, cannot be an efficient cause of any thing. A principle which is not subject to dissection, having body and parts—a principle of configuration is not capable of being an active cause ; therefore, it only exists as a passive principle, depending entirely on an active principle for its existence. Now, if animal color can be contemplated as a cause, it must possess configurative properties ; and if it possess these properties, then it is an independent principle, capable of living and acting after the man is dead, or decomposed. If it is argued that each component part of the man becomes independent when decomposed, and that animal color is one of the component parts, then I would ask, why we cannot comprehend its existence, the same as other matter of which the body was made ? If this cannot be done, then it cannot be regarded other than a passive principle in which there is no power of action. Color, therefore, cannot be an efficient cause of the malignant prejudice of the whites against the blacks ; it is only an imaginary cause at the most. It serves only as a trait by which a principle is identified.

The true cause of this prejudice is slavery. Slavery partakes of the nature and efficiency of all, and every thing, that is bad on earth and in hell. Its effect in the character of prejudice, as displayed towards the colored people, fully sustains my position—that effects partake of their parent cause, both in nature and quantity ; for certainly, nothing short of every thing evil on earth and in hell, in the form and character of slavery could be capable of producing such prejudicial injuries, as those under which the colored people are doomed to suffer. It must be admitted, that slavery assumes a most vicious character in its exercise towards them. Never could a people exist under greater injuries, than those under which this people have existed in this country ; slavery, in its worst form, is the cause of all injury sustained by them. The system of slavery in its effects, is imposed on the injured party in two forms, or by two methods. The first method is, by a code of laws, originating in public sentiment, as in slave states. The other is, prejudice originating in the same, as it exists in free states. The first method is prejudicial, and partakes of the corruptions of public sentiment, which is corrupted by prejudice ; but prejudice, in that case, assumes the form of law, and, therefore, is not capable of inflicting such deep injuries, as when it exists without law. Because to all law there is a limitation, whether good or bad ; hence, so far as the laws of slave states are concerned, a limitation of suffering may be contemplated, even under their direct influence. However severe slave laws may be, and however faithfully executed according to their letter and spirit—though by them the cup of injury be lavished out in full measure upon the objects of its abuse to the extent of its power, still, the innate principles of the human mind, will cause it to transcend such legal abuse, where a *limitation* can be comprehended.

Legal codes, however oppressive, have never as yet been able to crush the aspiring principles of human nature. The real monster slavery, cannot long exist, where it is sustained by legal codes only ; it is forced to stand off, and is capable of imposing its shadow only, in comparison to what it is capable of doing by collateral aid. When public sentiment, therefore, has become so morally, civilly, and politically corrupted by the principles of slavery, as to be determined in crushing the objects of its malignity, it is under the necessity of calling prejudice to its aid, as an auxiliary to its adopted formal code of wickedness, clothed like a semi-devil, with all the innate principles of the old dragon himself. This auxiliary, is all powerfully capable of accommodating itself to local circumstances and conditions, and appearing with all the nature of the old beast, slavery ; it is always ready to destroy every aspiration to civil, political and moral elevation, which arises in the breast of the oppressed. There is no pretext too absurd, by which to justify the expenditures of its soul-and-body-destroying energies. The complexion, features, pedigree, customs, and even the attributes and purposes of God, are made available to its justification.

By this monster, the withering influence of slavery is directed to the very vitals of the colored people—withering every incentive to improvement—rendering passive all the faculties of the intellect—subjecting the soul to a morbid state of insensibility —destroying the body—making one universal wreck of the best work of nature's God.

Such is its effect at the south, and scarcely less destructive at the north. The only difference is this : at the north, there is not so formal a code of laws by which to direct the energies of prejudice as at the south; still the doctrine of *expediency* full well makes up the deficiency of cruel laws, giving prejudice as full toleration to exercise itself, and in lavishing out its withering influence, as law at the south.

It is a remarkable fact that the moment the colored people show signs of life—any indication of being possessed with redeeming principles, that moment an unrelenting hatred arises in the mind which is inhabited by that foul fiend, prejudice ; and the possessor of it will never be satisfied, until those indications are destroyed ; space, time, nor circumstance, is no barrier to its exercise. Transplant the object of its malignity to Africa, or Canada, or elsewhere, and its poison is immediately transferred from local into national policy, and will exert all possible means it possesses, to accomplish its fell design. It always aims its deadly fangs at the noble and active principles of the immortal mind, which alone enables man to stand forth pre-eminent in all the works of God.*

Let the oppressed assume the character of capable men in buisness, either mercantile, mechanical, or agricultural,—let them assume the right of exercising themselves in the use of the common privileges of the country—let them claim the right of enjoying liberty, in the general acceptation of the term— let them exercise the right of speech and of thought—let them presume to enjoy the privileges of the sanctuary and the Bible let their souls be filled with glory and of God, and wish to bow the knee at the sacred altar, and commemorate the dying love of Christ the Lord—let them seek a decent burial for their departed friend in the church yard—and they are immediately made to feel that they are as a carcass destined to be preyed upon by the eagles of persecution. Thus they are followed from life's dawn to death's-doom.

I have no language wherewith to give slavery, and its auxiliaries, an adequate description, as an efficient cause of the miseries it is capable of producing. It seems to possess a kind of omnipresence. It follows its victims in every avenue of life.

The principle assumes still another feature equally destructive. It makes the colored people subserve almost every foul purpose imaginable. Negro or nigger, is an approbrious term, employed to impose contempt upon them as an inferior race, and also to express their deformity of person. Nigger lips, nigger shins, and nigger heels, are phrases universally common among the juvenile class of society, and full well understood by them ; they are early learned to think of these expressions, as they are intended to apply to colored people, and as being expressive or descriptive of the odious qualities of their mind and body. These impressions received by the young, grow with their growth, and strengthen with their strength. The term in itself, would be perfectly harmless, were it used only to distinguish one class of society from another ; but it is not used with that intent ; the practical definition is quite different in England to what it is here, for here, it flows from the fountain of purpose to injure. It is this baneful seed which is sown in the tender soil of youthful minds, and there cultivated by the hand of a corrupt immoral policy.

The universality of this kind of education is well known to the observing. Children in infancy receive oral instruction from the nurse. The first lessons given are, Johnny, Billy, Mary,

* Take Hayti for an example.

Sally, (or whatever the name may be,) go to sleep, if you
don't the old *nigger* will care you off; don't you cry—Hark;
the old *niggers'* coming—how ugly you are, you are worse
than a little *nigger*. This is a specimen of the first lessons
given.

The second is generally given in the domestic circle; in
some families it is almost the only method of correcting their
children. To inspire their half grown misses and masters to
improvement, they are told that if they do this or that, or if
they do thus and so, they will be poor or ignorant as a *nigger;*
or that they will be black as a *nigger;* or have no more credit
than a *nigger;* that they will have hair, lips, feet, or something of the kind, like a *nigger.* If doubt is entertained by
any, as to the truth of what I write, let them travel twenty
miles in any direction in this country, especially in the free
States, and his own sense of hearing will convince him of its
reality.

See nigger's thick lips—see his flat nose—nigger eye shine
—that slick looking nigger—nigger, where you get so much
coat?—that's a nigger priest—are sounds emanating from little
urchins of Christain villagers, which continually infest the
feelings of colored travellers, like the pestiferous breath of
young devils; and full grown persons, and sometimes professors of religion, are not unfrequently heard to join in the
concert.

A third mode of this kind of instruction is not altogether
oral. Higher classes are frequently instructed in school rooms
by refering them to the nigger-seat, and are sometimes threat-
ened with being made to sit with the niggers, if they do not
behave.

The same or similar use is made of nigger pews or seats in
meeting-houses. Professing Christians, where these seats exist,
make them a test by which to ascertain the amount of their
humility. This I infer from their own language; for, say they,
of the colored people, if we are only humble enough, we
should be willing to sit any where to hear the word. If our
hearts were right we should not care where we sit—I had as
lief sit there (meaning the nigger pew,) as any where in the
world. This, I admit, is all very good, but comes with rather
bad grace. But, as I above observed, this kind of education is
not altogether oral. Cuts and placards descriptive of the ne-
groe's deformity, are every where displayed to the observation
of the young, with corresponding broken lingo, the very character of which is marked with design.

6

Many of the popular book stores, in commercial towns and cities, have their show-windows lined with them. The bar-rooms of the most popular public houses in the country, sometimes have their ceiling literally covered with them. This display of American civility is under the daily observation of every class of society, even in New England. But this kind of education is not only systematized, but legalized. At the south, public newspapers are teeming through the country, bearing negro cuts, with remarks corresponding to the object for which they are inserted.

But this system is not carried on without deep design. It has hitherto been a settled opinion of philosophers that a black man could endure the heat better than a white man. Traders in human flesh have ever taken the advantage of that opinion, by urging it as a plea of justification of their obtaining Africans, as laborers in warm climates; hence, we may naturally expect, that in a slave country like this, it would be a universally admitted axiom; and the more readily admitted, as it is easily construed into a plea to justify their wicked purposes. If the black can endure the heat, and the white cannot, say they, it must be that God made him on purpose for that; hence, it is no harm for us to act in accordance with the purposes of God, and make him work. These are the simple inferences drawn from the philosophical premises, the justness of which I shall hereafter examine.

The arguments founded on these premises, are many. Cotton, rice, indigo, tobacco, and sugar, are great blessings to the world, say they, and they may as well be made to make them as not; for they are a lazy crew at the best, and if they are not made to work for us, they will not work at all, &c. But to come at the truth, the whole system is founded in avarice. I believe the premises to be the production of modern philosophy, bearing date with European slavery; and it has been the almost sole cause of the present prevailing public sentiment in regard to the colored population. It has given rise to the universal habit of thinking that they were made for the sole end of being slaves and underlings. There could be nothing more natural, than for a slaveholding nation to indulge in a train of thoughts and conclusions that favored their idol, slavery. It becomes the interest of all parties, not excepting the clergy, to sanction the premises, and draw the conclusions, and hence, to teach the rising generation. What could accord better with the objects of this nation in reference to blacks, than to teach their little ones that a negro is part monkey?

' The love of money is the root of all evil ; ' it will induce
its votaries to teach lessons to their little babes, which only fits
them for the destroyers of their species in this world, and for
the torments of hell in the world to come. When clergymen,
even, are so blinded by the god of this world, as to witness the
practice of the most heinous blasphemy in the house, said to
be dedicated to God, for centuries, without raising their warn-
ing voice to the wicked, it would not be at all surprising if they
were to teach their children a few lessons in the science of
anatomy, for the object of making them understand that a negro
is not like a white man, instead of teaching them his catechism.

The effect of this instruction is most disastrous upon the
mind of the community ; having been instructed from youth
to look upon a black man in no other light than a slave, and
having associated with that idea the low calling of a slave, they
cannot look upon him in any other light. If he should chance
to be found in any other sphere of action than that of a slave,
he magnifies to a monster of wonderful dimensions, so large
that they cannot be made to believe that he is a man and a
brother. Neither can they be made to believe it would be
safe to admit him into stages, steam-boat cabins, and tavern
dining-rooms; and not even into meeting-houses, unless he
have a place prepared on purpose. Mechanical shops, stores,
and school rooms, are all too small for his entrance as a man ;
if he be a slave, his corporeality becomes so diminished as to
admit him into ladies' parlors, and into small private carria-
ges, and elsewhere, without being disgustful on account of his
deformity, or without producing any other discomfiture. Thus
prejudice seems to possess a magical power, by which it makes
a being appear most odious one moment, and the next, beauti-
ful—at one moment too large to be on board a steam-boat, the
next, so small as to be convenient almost any where.

But prejudice is destructive to life. The public have been
frequently told the operation of the slave system is destructive
to the life of its victim ; this statement is intended generally to
be confined to those parts where slavery is legalized; and what
has been said relative to the subject is but a beginning of the
story. Indeed, I may say the publishers of the horrible effects
of slavery in this country, have not generally had the means of
knowing one half of its enormity. The extent of it will probably remain a secret until the great day of eternity. Many of
us who are conversant with fugitive slaves, on their arrival to
the free states, have an opportunity of hearing a tale of wo,
which for the want of adequate language, we are not able to

describe. These stories are told with so much native simplicity as to defy the most stubborn incredulity of the incredulous. But, though slavery in this way is carrying its thousands into eternity, in the southern states, yet it is doing hardly less so in the free states, as it displays itself in the character and form of prejudice.

Mind acts on matter. Contemplate the numerous free people of color under the despotic reign of prejudice—contemplate a young man in the ardor of youth, blessed with a mind as prolific as the air, aspiring to eminence and worth—contemplate his first early hopes blasted by the frost of prejudice—witness the ardor of youth inspiring him to a second and third trial, and as often repelled by this monster foe—hear him appealing to the laws of the land of his birth for protection—the haughty executives of the law spurning him from the halls of justice. He betakes to the temple of God—the last alternative around which his fading, dying hopes are hovering —but here, also, he receives a death thrust, and that by the hand of the priest of the altar of God. Yes—hear ye priests of the altar—it is the death thrust of slavery carried to the hearts of its victims by you. Yes—let it be known to the world, that the colored people who have been stolen, and have lost all allegiance to Africa, are sold in the shambles, and scouted from every privilege that makes life desirable. Under these discouragements they betake themselves to those who are called to preach good tidings to the meek, to bind up the broken-hearted, to proclaim liberty to the captives, and the opening of the prison doors to them that are bound, and they are set at nought by them also. The effect of these discouragements are every where manifest among the colored people.

I will venture to say, from my own experience and observation, that hundreds of them come to an untimely grave, by no other disease than that occasioned by oppression. And why should it be otherwise? They are virtually denied all possessions on earth, and how can they stay without a place whereon to rest.

I, as an individual, have have had sufficient opportunity to know something about prejudice, and its destructive effects. At an early period of my life, I was extensively engaged in mechanism, associated with a number of other colored men of master spirits and great minds. The enterprise was followed for about twenty years, perseveringly, in direct opposition to public sentiment, and the tide of popular prejudice. So intent were the parties in carrying out the principles of intelligent,

active free men, that they sacrificed every thing of comfort and
ease to the object. The most rigid economy was adhered to
at home and abroad. A regular school was established for the
instruction of the youth connected with the factory, and the
strictest rules of morality were supported with surprising assi-
duity; and ardent spirits found no place in the establishment.
After the expenditure of this vast labor and time, together
with many thousand dollars, the enterprise ended in a total
failure. By reason of the repeated surges of the tide of prejudice, the establishment, like a ship in a boisterous hurricane at
sea, went beneath its waves, richly laden, well manned, and
well managed, and all sunk to rise no more. Such was the
interest felt by the parties concerned, and such was their
sense of the need of such an establishment for the benefit of
colored youth, that they might acquire trades and a corresponding education, that they exerted every nerve to call it into
the notice of the public, that the professed friends of the colored people might have an opportunity to save it from becoming a wreck; but all in vain; prejudice had decreed its fate.
It fell, and with it fell the hearts of several of its undertakers
in despair, and their bodies into their graves.

With the above, I could record the names of scores whose
dissolution can be traced to a cloud of obstructions thrown in
their way to prevent enterprise.

I should proceed no farther with this tale of wo, were I
satisfied I had done my duty in the case. But the condition of
the colored people is such, even in the free states, that every
effort, however feeble, should he made to redeem them from
the influence of that dreadful monster—prejudice. I have
recently travelled among them as a missionary, and their condition is truly lamentable. Their immortal interests, as well as
their temporal, are in many places almost entirely disregarded;
and in others, their warmest friends seem not to comprehend
their true condition. I found several hundreds in some places,
who, though the bowl of knowledge was overflowing around
them, were not permitted to partake, without they receive it
from the cup of contempt, the thought of which, to sensitive
minds, is like a draught of wormwood and gall.

Slavery, in the form and character of prejudice, is as fatal,
yea, more fatal than the pestilence. It possesses imperial dominion over its votaries and victims. It demands and receives
homage from priests and people. It drinks up the spirit of the
church, and gathers blackness, and darkness, and death, around
her brow. Its poison chills the life blood of her heart. Its

gigantic tread on the Sabbath day, pollutes the altars of the
sanctuary of the Most High.   It withholds the word of life
from thousands of perishing immortals, and shuts the gate of
heaven alike upon those whose hearts it possesses, and those
marked out for its victims.   It opens wide the way to hell;
and as though posessed with more than magic power, coerces
its millions down to the pit of wo in defiance of the benevolence of a God, and the dying groans of a Saviour.   O Prejudice, thou art slavery in disguise ! and couldst thou ascend
to heaven, thy pestiferous breath would darken and poison that
now healthful and happy clime ; and thou wouldst make its
inhabitants feel the pains of the lowest hell.   If there are degrees of intensity to the misery of the damned, that being must
feel it in eternity, in whose heart prejudice reigned in this
world.   O Prejudice, I cannot let thee pass without tel ing
thee and thy possessors, that thou art a compound of all evil—
of all the corrupt passions of the heart.   Yea, thou art a participant in all the purposes of the wicked one—thou art the
very essence of hell.

CHAPTER IV.

ON THE CLAIMS OF THE COLORED PEOPLE TO ALL THE CIVIL, RELIGIOUS, AND SOCIAL PRIVILEGES OF THIS COUNTRY.

This proposition is in part embraced within the province of those of a preceding chapter. In following it, therefore, I shall be able to fulfil a promise therein contained.

The claims set up are founded in the fact that they are Americans by birth and blood. Complexion has never been made the legal test of citizenship in any age of the world. It has been established generally by birth and blood, and by purchase, or by the ceding of a province or territory from one nation to another. But as they are denied those privileges principally on the ground of their complexion and blood, it shall be my business in this concluding chapter to show—that though their complexion is as truly American as the complexion of the whites, yet it has nothing to do in settling the question. If blood has any thing to do with it, then we are able to prove that there is not a drop of African blood, according to the general acceptation of the term, flowing in the veins of an American born child, though black as jet. Children of African parents, recently arrived in this country, who have not undergone what is called seasoning, may partake of the characteristics of its African parents; such as the hair, complexion, and such like appendages, but the child's blood has nothing African about it, and for the following reasons. The blood of the parents in seasoning to this climate becomes changed—also, the food of the mother being the production of this country, and congenial to the climate—the atmosphere she breathes—the surrounding objects which strike her senses—all are principles which establish and give character to the constitutional principles of the child, among which the blood is an essential constituent; hence every child born in America, even if it be as black as jet, is American by birth and blood. The kind of root called Irish potatoes, is in truth American, if the potatoes are the production of American soil; and thus remain American potatoes, though they be red or deep scarlet. Some eagle-eyed philosophers, who possess great acuteness of smelling powers, think there is a difference of smell between the Africans and Europeans. Suppose that idea to be correct—would it prove any difference of smell between Americans who are constitutionally alike, and whose corporeals are sustained by the same aliment? In philosophically contemplating those constitutional properties, the color of the skin can no more be included than that of the eyes or the length of the nose.

It is the settled opinion of most people in this country, as I mentioned in a former chapter, that black Americans can endure the heat better than white Americans. This opinion is founded in the fact that black will retain heat while white emits it. I admit the proposition, but I doubt the correctness of the conclusions with respect to the color of animals.

Some minerals and dye-stuffs, and other black substances, will retain heat, which is owing to their not possessing any reflecting ingredient or property, by which the light or heat is thrown back. Heated iron will retain heat longer than heated brass, for the same reason—i. e. iron is not possessed of as much reflection as brass—or in other words, it has not the properties of reflection. I believe these are the considerations, and these only, that are capable of sustaining the proposition.

But these considerations do not and cannot embrace those connected with animal color, for that has neither the power of retaining nor emiting heat—and for the very good reason it possesses no properties; hence no efficient cause in itself to produce any effect whatever. The principle as it exists in relation to minerals and other substances, depends entirely upon the nature of the properties of which these several bodies are composed; but can the principle be made to apply to animal color?

Analyze black iron, and black properties are found in the iron. Analyze black dye-stuff, and black properties are found in the stuff. Analyze light brass, and light reflecting properties are found in the brass.

Analyze a black man, or anatomize him, and the result of research is the same as analyzing or anatomizing a white man.

Before the dissecting knife passes half through the outer layer of the skin, it meets with the same solids and fluids, and from thence all the way through the body. Now I should like to have some modern philosophers, who have got more sense than common school-boys, to tell the world how it is that two bodies of matter, the one exactly similar to the other, in every minute principle of their composition, should produce different effect by the one emiting heat, and the other retaining it.

If it is contended that those properties exist- in the animal color itself, then, if they will be good enough to analyze it and give us a knowledge of its parts—i. e. if they think a black head can receive and understand it—they will do the world a great favor, as well as ourselves.

If the foregoing considerations are reconcilable, then it may be taken for granted that a black man can work better in the hot sun than a white man—but if they are not reconcilable, then the whole theory is only calculated to dupe the black people, and make knaves of the white people.

But to return. The colored people being constitutionally Americans, they are depending on American climate, American aliment, American government, and American manners, to sustain their American bodies and minds ; a withholding of the enjoyment of any American principle from an American man, either governmental, ecclesiastical, civil, social or alimental, is in effect taking away his means of subsistence ; and consequently, taking away his life. Every ecclesiastical body which denies an American the privilege of participating in its benefits, becomes his murderer. Every state which denies an American a citizenship with all its benefits, denies him his life. Every community which denies an American the privilege of public conveyances, in common with all others, murders him by piece-meal. Every community which withholds social intercourse with an American, by which he may enjoy current information, becomes his murderer of the worst kind. The claims the colored people set up, therefore, are the claims of an American.

They ask priests and people to withhold no longer their inalienable rights to seek happiness in the sanctuary of God, at the same time and place that other Americans seek happiness. They ask statesmen to open the way whereby they, in common with other Americans, may aspire to honor and worth as statesmen—to place their names with other Americans—subject to a draft as jurymen and other functionary appointments, according to their ability. They ask their white American brethren to think of them and treat them as American citizens,

7

and neighbors, and as members of the same American family. They urge their claims in full assurance of their being founded in immutable justice. They urge them from a sense of patriotism, from an interest they feel in the well being of their common country. And lastly, they urge them from the conviction that God, the judge of all men, will avenge them of their wrongs, unless their claims are speedily granted.

There are some objections urged against these claims. One is, that the greater part of the colored people are held as property, and if these claims are granted, their owners would be subject to great loss. In answer to this objection, I would remark, that were I to accede to the right of the master to his property in man, still I should conceive the objection groundless, for it is a well known fact that a far greater portion of the colored people who are free, purchased their freedom, and the freedom of their families. Many of them have purchased themselves several times over. Thousands of dollars have been paid over to masters annually, which was the proceeds of extra labor, in consideration of their expected freedom. My colored acquaintances are numerous who have thus done, some of whom were under the necessity of running away to obtain their freedom after all.

I am sufficiently acquainted with the sentiments and views of the slave population of every slave state in the union, to warrant me in the conclusion, that if the despotic power of the master was wrested from him, and the slaves placed under a law of ever so rigid a nature, with the privilege of paying for themselves by their extra labor, there would be comparatively few slaves in the country in less than seven years. The most of them would pay the round price of their bodies, and come out freemen.

Another objection is, that the slaves, if freed at once, would not be capable of enjoying suffrages.

This objection has less foundation than the former, for the several state legislatures of the slave states are continually assisting the masters to keep them in ignorance, and why not legislate in favor of their being informed?

Some contend that they are not now fit for freedom, but ought to be prepared and then freed.

Such a calculation is preposterous. We might as well talk about educating a water machine to run against its propelling power, as to talk about educating a slave for a free man. When travelling through the state of New York, recently, I made some inquiries with respect to the colored people, who in some

places are very numerous. I was there informed, by gentlemen whose veracity I cannot doubt, that they are generally in-
dolent and dissipated, far worse than they were when they were
slaves. I was told also, that many of them had enjoyed excellent opportunities to become wealthy and respectable. That
before the Emancipation Bill was passed in that state, they
were mostly slaves, but had an opportunity of obtaining an excellent education, and the art of farming, equal, and in many
instances, superior to most white men. When they became
free, many of their masters, as a reward of former faithfulness,
furnished them with means to operate for themselves on a small
scale. My informants expressed much astonishment at the
fact that most of those who had the best opportunity to do well,
had become dissipated, and much worse in character and conduct than when they were slaves.

I have introduced this narrative for the purpose of showing
that slaves cannot be educated for free men. A slave is meta-
morphosed into a machine, adapted to a specific operation, and
propelled by the despotic power of the slave system, without any
motive to attract. The influence of this power acts upon a
slave the same as upon any other biased agent. By the abro-
gation of the propelling cause of all the acts of the machine, it
ceases to move. The slave is now left, without either motive
to attract, or power to coerce. A slave, as such, in undergoing the change from a moral, intelligent being, to a mere machine, lost all the innate principles of a freeman. Hence, when
the principles of slavery ceases to act upon him, to the end for
which he is a slave, he is left a mere out-of-use wreck of ma-
chinery ; under nothing but the withering influence of the pelt-
ing rain of wickedness.

It is true, many of the slaves of New York had some education, but that education was acquired when a slave. Hence, it
was only a collateral means by which he was rendered a more
efficient machine. His education was the education of a slave,
and not a freeman.

These conclusions may be thought by some to go against the
doctrine of immediate abolition—not so. The doctrine of immediate abolition embraces the idea of an entire reversal of
the system of slavery. The work of emancipation is not complete when it only cuts off some of the most prominent limbs of
slavery, such as destroying the despotic power of the master,
and the laying by of the cow-hide. The man who fell among
thieves was emancipated in that way. His cruel captivators,
I suppose, thought they had done a great act of philanthropy

when they left off beating him. But their sort of emancipation left the poor man half dead—precisely in the same way New York emancipated her slaves, after beating them several hundred years, left them, half dead, without proscribing any healing remedy for the bruises and wounds received by their maltreatment. But the good Samaritan had quite a different view of the subject. It is remembered, undoubtedly, that before he acted, there were several who passed by that way, saw the man, but passed by on the other side. Whether they were Unionists, Colonizationists, or Abolitionists, every one must judge for themselves. But when the good man came along, he carried out the principles of immediate abolitionism. If New York had imitated him, there would have been no complaint about her emancipated negroes (as they are called,) being worse than when they were slaves.

I repeat, that emancipation embraces the idea that the emancipated must be placed back where slavery found them, and restore to them all that slavery has taken away from them. Merely to cease beating the colored people, and leave them in their gore, and call it emancipation, is nonsense. Nothing short of an entire reversal of the slave system in theory and practice—in general and in particular—will ever accomplish the work of redeeming the colored people of this country from their present condition.

Let the country, then, no longer act the part of the thief. Let the free states no longer act the part of them who passed by on the other side, and leaving the colored people half dead, especially when they were beaten by their own hands, and so call it emancipation—raising a wonderment why the half dead people do not heal themselves. Let them rather act the part of the good Samaritan. That only will open an effectual door through which sympathies can flow, and by which a reciprocity of sentiment and interest can take place — a proper knowledge acquired by the benefactor relative to his duty, and reciprocated on the part of the benefited.

This state of things would possess redeeming power. Every collateral means would be marshaled under the heaven-born principle, that requires all men to do unto others as they would that others should do unto them. It would kindle anew the innate principles of moral, civil and social manhood, in the down-trodden colored Americans ; bidding them arise as from the dead, and speed their way back to the height from whence they have fallen. Nor would the call be in vain. A corresponding action on their part would respond to the cheering voice. The countenance which has been cast down, hitherto, would brighten up with joy. Their narrow foreheads, which have hitherto been contracted for the want of mental exercise, would begin to broaden. Their eye balls, hitherto strained out to prominence by a frenzy excited by the flourish of the whip, would fall back under a thick foliage of curly eyebrows, indicative of deep penetrating thought. Those muscles, which have hitherto been distended by grief and weeping, would become contracted to an acuteness, corresponding to that acuteness of perception with which business men are blessed. That interior region, the dwelling place of the soul, would be lighted up with the fires of love and gratitude to their benefactors on earth, and to their great Benefactor above, driving back those clouds of slavery and of prejudice which have hitherto darkened and destroyed its vision. And thus their whole man would be redeemed, rendering them fit for the associates of their fellow men in this life, and for the associates of angels in the world to come.

Sons of Columbia, up get ye;
Purge you from slavery's guilty stain,
Defend the honest poor, the truth maintain.

Sons of pilgrim sires, up get ye;
Purge you from slavery's guilty stain,
Your country's stained with blood all o'er the main.

Priests of the altar, up get ye;
Purge you from slavery's guilty stain,
Cease to be slavery's vassals—dupes to gain.

Priests of the altar up get ye;
Purge you from slavery's guilty stain,
No more the holy name of God profane.

Priests of the altar, up get ye;
Purge you from slavery's guilty stain,
Come ye from under slavery's prejudicial reign.

Priests of the altar, up get ye;
Purge you from slavery's guilty stain,
The trump of God has sounded—Hark—it sounds again.

Daughters of freedom, up get ye;
Purge you from slavery's guilty stain,
Shall violated chastity call for help in vain?

Daughters of freedom, up get ye;
Purge you from slavery's guilty stain,
Ere thy sisters' grief 'gainst thee in heaven complain.

Statesmen of Columbia, up get ye;
Hark! Jefferson presuag'd from first,
Trembling for his country—proclaimed—God is just!!

Priests and people, all, up get ye;
Hark! hear the prophets tell,
How nations forgetting God are sent to hell.

Priests and people, all, up get ye;
Purge you from that dreadful sin,
Prejudice—of dev'lish extract—hellish fiend.

Priests and people, all, up get ye;
Repent ye while you may,
An awful judgment is at hand—God's vengeful day.

☞The sermon, as proposed in our title page, is omitted on the account that it would swell the work far beyond our calculation. It will accompany a work entitled Easton's Lectures on Civil, Social, and Moral Economy, which will be presented to the public in a few weeks. The surplus proceeds of that work, as well as of this, after their expenses are paid, will be given to a colored society in Hartford, Con., who have lost their meeting-house by fire.

An extensive supply of this work may be had by forwarding an order to Isaac Knapp's Book Store and Liberator Office, No. 25 Cornhill, at the rate of $18 per 100—$2.50 per doz. 25 cents single copy. Subscribers for the other work solicited on the same conditions—directed to the same office before the first of April.

Wherein the works are deficient in their claims to patronage, it is hoped will be made up by the claims of the suffering society, for whom the proceeds are intended.

ERRATA.

6th page, 6th line from the top, instead of 'sprung' read 'springing' —and for 'you may find' read 'are found.'

10th page, 2d paragraph, 6th line, instead of 'conquest of armies' read 'conquest in arms'—also, 3d paragraph, 6th line, instead of 'impossible' read 'improbable.'

11th page, 1st line, instead of 'learning' read 'litany.'

12th page, 3d line, instead of 'by conveyance' read 'by *other* conveyance,'—also, instead of 'kindred and' &c. read 'subjects or' &c.—and for 'defender' read 'defendants.'

14th page, last paragraph, 2d line, instead of 'have annual,' &c. read 'receive annual,' &c.

18th page, 3d paragraph, 5th line, instead of 'the superiority' read 'the *pretended* superiority.'

19th page, 9th line from the top, read after 'and,' '*their country*' virtually, &c.

24th page, 2d paragraph, two last lines, instead of 'their progenitors since that period,' read 'since the commencement of that period.'

26th page, 2d paragraph, 12th line, instead of 'pangs' read 'fangs.'

28th page, 3d, 4th, 5th and 6th lines from the bottom, read thus: 'In convoking the Continental Congress of the 4th of September, 1774, there was not a word said about color. At a subsequent period, Congress met again, and agreed to get in readiness 12,000 men, to act in any emergency; also, a request was' &c.

31st page, 4th paragraph, 1st line, instead of 'Moble' read 'Mobile.'

34th page, 7th line from the top, for 'halo' read 'halloo.'

45th page, 5th line from the top, instead of 'surprising' read 'unsurpassing.'

WILLIAM J. WATKINS

*Our Rights as Men. An Address Delivered in Boston,
Before the Legislative Committee on the Militia,
February 24, 1853*

OUR RIGHTS AS MEN.

AN ADDRESS

DELIVERED IN BOSTON, BEFORE THE

Legislative Committee on the Militia,

FEBRUARY 24, 1853,

BY

WILLIAM J. WATKINS,

IN BEHALF OF SIXTY-FIVE COLORED PETITIONERS, PRAYING FOR A
CHARTER TO FORM AN

Independent Military Company.

BOSTON:
PRINTED BY BENJAMIN F. ROBERTS,
No. 19 WASHINGTON STREET.

PREFACE.

~~~~~~~~~~~~~~~~

WHEN the Author wrote the following Address, nothing could have been more foreign to his expectations, than to behold it sent forth upon the wings of the wind.

Should it fall into the hand of the Critic, he will, therefore, lay down *pro tempore*, his weapons, and

"pass my imperfections by."

The Author is not a man of war. He thinks the Apostolic injunction, "Be at peace with all men," should elicit universal and implicit obedience. These pages are a vindication of our RIGHTS AS CITIZENS, not a discourse upon our DUTY AS CHRISTIANS. A military Hero is not his *beau ideal* of a Christian, but *vice versa*. The vocation of Beelzebub, is to "scatter, tear and slay;" that of Man, to "deal justly, love mercy, and walk humbly before God." At least, so thinks the

AUTHOR.

ADDRESS.

Mr. Chairman and Gentlemen:

It is with unaffected diffidence and extreme reluctance, that I appear before you in the present capacity; and my diffidence and reluctance are induced by a multiplicity of considerations. The arduous duties of my vocation, aside from others of an extraneous nature, have precluded the possibility of that due preparation, I consider necessary for one of my youth and consequent inexperience, to appear before your honorable body. Another consideration, gentlemen, is a consciousness of my inability to bring the subject before you with that force and perspicuity of style, which would, doubtless, elicit in its behalf, an intensity of interest commensurate with its nature and importance.

Laboring, Gentlemen, under those crushing disabilities to which my complexion has made me liable, I have never dived very deeply into the Artesian well of Science; I have never been able to "talk with the thunder as friend to friend, or weave my garland from the lightning's wing ;".I have been denied those educational advantages of which the more favored race have been and still are the recipients. But although I cannot bring into requisition that profundity of thought, that logical acumen, that elegance of diction, of which you, gentlemen, are capable, this fact does not, in the least, derogate from the truthfulness of the sentiments I shall endeavor to advance, nor does it detract from their acceptability.

We have come here to-day, to deal not in rhyme and rhetoric, but in plain matter-of-fact, in sober reality. We have come, Mr. Chairman, to tell you what we want: why such a petition as this has been presented to the Honorable Body of whom you form a part, and why, in our opinion, such a petition should be granted. We have come before you, trusting in the inherent righteousness of our cause, and the justice which should, and which doubtless will, characterize your honorable body; and we trust our prayer will be effectual.

Mr. Chairman, I shall endeavor to-day to argue the general merits of this question, according to the measure of my ability. I would not, were I able, intrude upon the vocation of my learned friend, by discussing the question in its legal bearings, I leave that for a wiser head, and a tongue more eloquent. And while I stand up to represent those with whom I am proud to be identified, I respectfully solicit you, gentlemen, to regard us not as obsequious suppliants for favor, but as men, proud of, and conscious of the inherent dignity of manhood; as men, who, knowing our rights, dare, at all hazards, to maintain them. You know, gentlemen, every one of you, that we, as a people, are the victims of a cruel and relentless spirit of caste. The Juggernaut of American Prejudice would feign crush the manhood out of us, and place us in the category of the vilest of the vile; aye, with the brutes that perish; but we are, nevertheless, men; men, whether you regard our mental, moral, or physical conformation; and all we demand of you, is, that we be treated as men; that we be dealt with as all law-abiding citizens; and God will take care of the consequences, let those consequences be what they may.

Mr. Chairman,—In addressing you for a few moments, let us inquire,

1st. INTO THE NATURE OF THE PETITION.

2ndly. INTO THE CHARACTER OF THE PETITIONERS.

3rdly. WHY SHOULD THE PETITION BE GRANTED?

4thly. WE WILL NOTICE, BRIEFLY, THE HAPPY RESULTS CONSEQUENT UPON GRANTING IT.

First, then, THE NATURE OF THE PETITION.

"To the Honorable Senate and House of Representatives, of the Commonwealth of Massachusetts.

"We, the undersigned, citizens of Boston and vicinity, respectfully pray for a Charter to form an Independent Military Company."

Surely, gentlemen, there can be nothing unreasonable in the nature of this Petition. Nothing, absolutely nothing; nothing generally, nothing particularly. If there is, gentlemen, I am utterly unable to discern it. But, possibly, it is for the scriptural reason that "the light shineth in the darkness, and the darkness comprehendeth it not. We merely ask for a Charter to form an Independent Military Company; such a one as has been granted to a company of white citizens. We ask, Sir, that the Old Bay State will throw around us its protecting arm. We know that by wishing to be treated as men, we shall elicit the vindictive anathemas of a few, who live daily and hourly on the pap of American prejudice; but none of these things move us, if Massachusetts but gather us together as a hen gathereth her brood under her wings. We might, with propriety, have petitioned your honorable body, that we be enrolled among the General Militia; that the same immunities be extended towards us, that are extended towards other citizens of Massachusetts, irrespective of complexional distinction and physical peculiarities.

But we do not wish you to understand us as acquiescing in the righteousness of the prospective principle, because we ask for your protection in the exercise and enjoyment of a *portion* of our rights as men; for we are entitled to ALL the rights and immunities of CITIZENS OF MASSACHUSETTS. Thank God, this is the Age of Progress, not Retrogression. We are content now, for certain reasons, to ask for a Charter to form an Independent Company; a State Company, if you please. You, gentlemen, certainly cannot consider this as presumption. If you grant us this Petition, there is nothing in the nature of it, that will tend directly or indirectly to the dissolution of the Federal Union. For we are, *de facto*, a State Company, an Independent Company, segregated from the rest of mankind, and not in a position to cause the hair of our loving brethren of the Georgia Fusileers, or the South Carolina Dragoons, to "stand on end like quills upon the fretful porcupine," because, like them, we are enrolled among the General Militia, and liable to be called upon, when they

proscription

are summoned, to defend our lives, our fortunes and our sacred honors.

Having briefly noticed the nature of the Petition, and shown that there is nothing particularly dreadful and alarming about it, we will, in accordance with our arrangement, INQUIRE INTO THE CHARACTER OF THE PETITIONERS.

And who are they, Mr. Chairman? What is their character, gentlemen? In a word, they are among the most respectable men in the community. They are law-abiding, tax-paying, liberty-loving, NATIVE-BORN, AMERICAN CITIZENS; men who love their country, despite its heinous iniquities; iniquities piled up in dreadful agony to the heavens. I see arrayed in the List of Signers, men of affluence and education, of respectability and moral worth; men, in possession of those great and good qualities, the developement of which, exerts a healthy influence throughout the varied ramifications of society. They are men, Sir, that do honor to the State; as respectable in every point of view, as any list ever appended to a Petition, since "the morning stars sang together, and all the sons of God shouted for joy." And more than this, some of them are the descendants of revolution sires, and revolution mothers; the descendants of those, who, in those times that tried men's souls, counted not their lives dear unto them, but their blood flowed freely in defence of their country; they fought, they bled, they conquered; aye, they died, that we might live as FREEMEN. And shall we be excluded from the pale of humanity, denied those rights, left to us as a legacy by our fathers? Shall we be driven from the festive board, when all the world has been invited to come, and sit around the table? Yes! every nation, kindred, tongue and people! Forbid it Justice, forbid it Humanity, forbid it, ye spirits of our Fathers, now hovering over us, forbid it our country, forbid it Heaven!

Gentlemen, the very fact that some of these who have signed this Petition, are descendants of those who faced the cannon's mouth, and quaked not when it bellowed forth its dreadful thunders; who quailed not beneath its lurid lightnings, and yet are denied rights and privileges accorded to the descendants of those who shot down the brave patriots of the revolution, should be enough to cause the blood to boil within you, and cause "horror upon horror's head accumulate."

In presenting these petitioners before you, Mr. Chairman, in desribing their character, gentlemen, I have nothing extenuated, nor set down aught in hyperbolic phrase. They are just the men I represent them to be, and this being the case, your sense of right and your love of Justice forbid any other treatment of their Petition than one which can abide the test of manly criticism, and stand out in the blazing sunlight, eliciting the approbation of God, the admiration of angels, the approval of your own consciences, the plaudits of the world of Truth and Justice and Humanity. We beseech you, by the exalted character of those whom we have the honor to represent, by all that is noble, just and true therein, *"Hear us for our cause."*

In the third place, Gentlemen, WHY SHOULD THIS PETITION BE GRANTED?

It should be granted because the request is a reasonable one, and one emanating from a body of men who have an absolute right to demand it. We proceed, then, upon the assertion that we have an unrestricted right to the enjoyment of full civil privileges ; a right to demand and receive every thing which Massachusetts by her Bill of Rights, grants to her citizens, irrespective of any accidental or fortuitous circumstance, the contingency of birth, education, fortune, or complexion. We are men, and we wish to be treated, as men in the land of the Pilgrims should be treated. Mr. Chairman, the laws of this Commonwealth know no man by the color of his skin, the texture of his hair, or the symmetrical developement of his physical organism. It is too true, sir, that even here, American Prejudice, the inseparable concomitant of American Slavery, stands out in bold relief, the embodiment of Death, Hell, and the Grave ; the incarnation of a principle which had its origin in the council chamber of the lost, and one which is fostered only by those affiliated with the Prince of darkness. But, thank God, in the eye of the Law, we all, sir, stand upon one common platform. What have the colored people of this country done, that we should be treated as a hissing and a by-word, a pest and a nuisance, the off-scouring of the earth ?

When we cast our eyes abroad this vast Republic, a singular anomaly, a living paradox presents itself. Once, every year, in this land of the free, on Freedom's Natal day, the people assemble in public convocation, and in intonations loud and long, proclaim to the despotism of the world, " We hold these truths to be self-evident ; that all men are born free and created equal, and are endowed by their Cre-

ator, with certain inalienable rights, and among these are life, liberty,
and the pursuit of Happiness." Yes. Our jubilatic anthems roll over
the wide waste of waters, o'er hills and valleys, rivers, woods, and
plains ; and the burden of our song is, " We are free, We are free."

But hark ! for amid the rapturous symphonies of Freedom's song,
I hear a low sepulchral voice ; the voice of agony, of Rachel weeping for her children, and refusing to be comforted ; I also hear the
voice of the nominally free ; of men, women, and children, whose
Freedom (?) gives the lie to your song of Jubilee.   God grant the
murmurings of the crushed of this *soi-dissant* Republic, which roll towards Heaven like the voice of many waters, descend not in curses
upon the defenceless head of this great Nation ; that the lightnings
that now sleep side by side, with the thunders of God Almighty's
wrath, be not commissioned to strike the proud fabric of our glory,
and humble us in the dust.   Mr. Chairman, American Republicanism, and its loving hand-maid American Christianity (?) seem determined if there is any manhood in us, to crush it out of us.   We are
hunted like the partridge upon the mountain, persecuted, afflicted,
tormented.   You are the Jews, the chosen people of the Lord, and
we are the poor rejected Gentiles.   But the times of refreshing are
soon coming from the presence of the Lord, and we wait, with anxious
expectation, the arrival of this auspicious era; for then, we trust, the
fullness of the Gentiles will be brought in.

> " Fly swiftly round, ye wheels of Time,
> And bring the welcome day."

You talk about the caste of the Hindoo, &c.   Why, the Spirit of
caste, lives and breathes in this country, as though it were stamped
with the impress of imperishable vitality.

Your laws are founded in caste, conceived in caste, born in caste.
Caste is the God whom this great Nation delights to honor.   Caste
is in your singing, your preaching, your praying ; your *beau-ideal* of
Heaven is a place of unfading joy, and resplendent magnificence,
where you shall play for ever upon your golden harps, and the colored people, if they, like Uncle Tom, submit to your indignities with
Christian meekness and becoming resignation, shall be permitted,
from the Negro pew, to *peep into* the glory of your third heaven
to all eternity !

Gentlemen, only look at the picture. Your schools, and colleges, and stores, and pulpits, are all closed against us ; every avenue to honor and renown is piled up with mountains to obstruct our progress, and if we ever stand forth, a disenthralled people, we must burst a chain as long and broad as the ever grasping arm of this great country, and ten thousand times more solid than the compact which binds you together. *O tempora! O mores!* And then, to add insult to injury, we are gravely told that God has drawn a broad line of demarcation between us ; that we are inately inferior to the white man ; that we are in the language of a Rev. Colonizationist, " too low in our debasement, to be reached by the Heavenly light." And this precious divine, *et id omne genus*, tell us in the same breath, that we are the people to evangelize and christianize Africa. Yes ! with all our ignorance and degradation, we only are the people, the ordained people of the Lord. Truly " God moves in a mysterious way, His wonders to perform." How is it, that while we remain in this enlightened land, we are buried so low in the abyss of infamy, that the arm of God's omnipotence cannot resurrect us ? But, just go across the water, and be landed upon the shores of Africa, where, as Hon. Edward Everett, tells us, " Death sits portress at the undefended gateways of her mud-built villages, yellow and intermittent fevers, blue plagues, and poisons, that you can see as well as feel, await your approach ;" Yes ! if we land on these healthy shores, then, we become kings and priests unto God, and thrones and dominions and principalities and powers dance before our vision like dew-drops glittering before the king of day. Colonization does for us in Africa, what God cannot do for us in America. *Mirabile dictu!*

O wonderful efficacy of the Atlantic Ocean !! What wonderful power of transformation !!!

The departed Webster in making a Colonization speech, once said, we, (the whites) imitate the example of Abram and Lot ; when a difficulty had arisen between their respective herdsmen, said the former, " Let there be no strife, I pray thee, between me and thee. If thou wilt take the left hand, then I will go to the right." But the distinguished statesman did not get more than half way in his illustration. We are perfectly willing to accept from the U. States a similar proposition to the one offered by Abram. Let us read the whole of it. " Let there be no strife between us, we pray thee; between thy

✻

herdsmen, &c., &c., for we be brethren. Is not the whole land before thee? Separate thyself from me, I pray thee : If thou wilt go to the left hand, then I will go to the right; but if thou wilt go to the right hand, then I will go to the left. But, as Mr. Webster related the interesting colloquy, the proposition is of a jug-handle character.

If *you* will go to Africa, then *we* will stay in America, says Mr. W., and there stops ; but why not imitate the whole example, and say, "But if *you* will stay in America, then *we* will go to Africa." This reminds me of an anecdote you have doubtless heard before. A white man and an Indian once went in pursuit of game, and agreed prior to starting, that they would divide whatever game they might catch. When the expedition was over, they found that they had shot a wild goose, and a buzzard. They then proceeded to divide, according to agreement. Said the white man, "goose for me, and turkey buzzard for you, or turkey buzzard for you, and goose for me." "But," said the Indian, "you no say goose for me once."

Now, Mr. Chairman, we know who are our friends and who are our enemies. Yes, Gentlemen, despite our inate inferiority, notwithstanding the obliquity of our mental vision, our perceptions are sufficiently acute to discern iniquity whether we behold it arrayed in the habiliments of legislative wisdom, or enveloped beneath the garb of ministerial sanctity, and missionary zeal, or stalking abroad the land unmasked, in all its native hideousness, its heart-appalling deformity.

We ask no favors, Mr. Chairman, at the hands of our country; all we demand, is, the unrestricted right to breathe unmolested, the pure, unadulterated atmosphere of Heaven. We are told we cannot rise! Take the millstone from off our necks. We are inferior to the white man! *Give us our rights.* We can't be elevated in the land of our birth! Give us our rights, we ask no more. Treat us like men ; carry out the principles of your immortal declaration, " all men are born free, and created equal, and are endowed by their Creator with certain inalienable rights, and among these are life, liberty, and the pursuit of happiness," and *then*, if we do not equal you in every respect, let us be the recipients of your intensified hate, your vituperative anathemas; *then* let your ponderous Juggernaut roll on, or, like Nebuchadnezzar, let us be driven beyond the pale of Humanity, to herd with the beasts of the field. But do not blame us for occupying a position in which *you* have placed us. And all this Petition demands, is, that you place us in a position that we may command respect. You need not fear the consequences. Pull down the barrier that obstructs our progress ; hew down the mountains ; fill up the valleys ; make the crooked paths straight, and the rough places smooth, and then you may talk as long and loudly as you please, about the incapacity of the colored race. What says the Hon. Edward Everett, concerning our intellectual inferiority ?

It would, says he, " be unjust to urge, as a proof of the intellectual inferiority of the civilized men of color in this country, that they have not made much intellectual progress. It appears to me, that they have done quite as much as could be expected under the depressing circumstances in which they have been placed. What branch of the European family, if held in the same condition for three centuries, would not be subject to the same reproach ?" And now, Mr. Chairman, are we unworthy to elict the treatment due to man ; man created in the image of God, and stamped with the impress of Immortality ? In the language of the Apostle, I would exhort you, whatsoever things are true, whatsoever things are just, whatsoever things are honest, whatsoever things are lovely, and of good report, *think on these things.* I know that the majority of the nation have signed the deed which abrogates the right to *speak* on these things, but, gentlemen, you are yet at liberty to " *think* on these things," the requisitions of the compromise, the edict of the Baltimore Inquisition to the contrary notwithstanding. Why, gentlemen, should our Petition be granted ? or rather, why should it not be granted ? Gentlemen, of the Legislature may advance what ostensible reasons they please ; shewing why, in their opinion, it should not be, but to this conclusion they must come at last : " You are colored men, and you must not be elevated, you must not stand on equality with white men."

But, Sir, if colored men helped achieved *your* liberty as well as mine, if *your* fathers and my fathers found one common revolutionary grave, we ask you in the name of crushed and bleeding humanity, why should you, in point of privileges, like Capernaum of old, be elevated to heaven, and we be cast down to Hell ? No wonder Jefferson " trembled for his country, when he reflected that God is just, and his justice sleeps not forever." Why should *you* be a chosen people more than *we ?* The great poiniard of British tyranny, which was plunged in the heart of *your* Fathers, and caused their noble blood to flow so freely, brought the purple flood from *our* hearts also. We have referred to the fact of our Fathers' having fought to achieve this country's Independence. Allow me to quote in this connection, the eloquent words of a talented Reverend gentleman of Color, of the City of New York:—"We are NATIVES of this country : we ask only to be treated as well as FOREIGNERS. Not a few of our Fathers suffered and bled to purchase its Independence ; we ask only to be treated as well as those who fought against it. We have toiled to cultivate it, and to raise it to its present prosperous condition ; we ask only to share equal privileges with those who come from distant lands to enjoy the fruits of our labor." Yes! all we ask is, that you treat us as well as you do the Irish, German, Hungarian, aye, the whole host of them. We have adverted to the fact, that colored men fought for the Independence of this country. Allow me to read, in this connection, from Botta's " History of the Wars of the Independence of the United States of America."

"Meanwhile, at Boston, things assumed the most serious aspect. The inhabitants supported with extreme repugnance the presence of the soldiers ; and these detested the Bostonians. Hence, mutual insults and provocations occurred.

" 1770. Finally, on the morning of the 2d of March, as a soldier was passing by the premises of John Grey, a ropemaker, he was assailed with abusive words, and afterwards beaten severely. He soon returned, accompanied by some of his comrades. An affray ensued between the soldiers and the ropemakers, in which the latter had the worst.

" The *people* became greatly exasperated ; and, on the 5th of the same month, between seven and eight o'clock in the evening, a violent tumult broke out. The multitude, armed with clubs, ran towards King street, crying, ' *Let us drive out these ribalds ; they have no business here.*' The soldiers who were lodged in the barracks of Murray, were eager to fall upon the populace ; and their officers had the greatest difficulty in restraining them. Meanwhile, it was cried that the town had been set on fire ; the bells pealed alarm, and the crowd increased from all parts. The rioters rushed furiously towards the custom house ; they approached the sentinel, crying, ' *Kill him! kill him!*' They assaulted him with snow balls. pieces of ice, and whatever they could lay their hands upon. The sentinel in this conjuncture, having called the guard, Captain Preston detached a corporal and a few soldiers to protect this man, and the chest of the customs, from the popular fury. They marched with their arms loaded, and the captain himself followed; they encountered a band of the populace, *led* by a mulatto named Attucks, who brandished their clubs, and pelted them with snow balls. The maledictions, the imprecations, the execrations of the multitude, were horrible. In the midst of a torrent of invectives from every quarter, the military was challenged to fire. The detachment was surrounded; and the populace advanced to the points of their bayonets. The soldiers appeared like statues; the cries, the howlings, the menaces, the violent din of bells, still sounding the alarm, increased the confusion and the horrors of these moments; at length the mulatto and twelve of *his* companions, pressing forward, environed the soldiers, and striking their muskets with their clubs, cried to the multitude; ' *Be not afraid, they dare not fire; why do you hesitate. why do you not kill them, why not crush them at once?*' The mulatto lifted his arm against Captain Preston, and having turned one of the muskets, he seized the bayonet with his left hands, as if he intended to execute his threat. At this moment, confused cries were heard, ' *The wretches dare not fire.*' Firing succeeds; *Attucks is slain.* Two other discharges follow. Three were killed, five severely wounded; several others slightly; the greater part, persons that were passing by chance; or quiet spectators of this scene. Eight soldiers only fired, and none more than once. The populace dispersed, but returned soon after to carry off the dead and wounded."

I hold in my hand, sir, a Pamphlet, entitled " Services of Colored Americans, in the Wars of 1776 and 1812," by W. C. Nell, Esq., a colored gentleman, whose mental and moral qualifications are of the highest order. From this Pamphlet, I make the following quotations :

" The late Governor EUSTIS, of Massachusetts, the pride and boast of the democracy of the East, himself an active participant in the War, and therefore a most competent witness, states that the Free Colored Soldiers entered the ranks with the whites. The time of those who were Slaves was purchased of their masters, and they were induced to enter the service, in consequence of a law of Congress, by which, on condition of their serving in the ranks during the War, they were made Freemen. This hope of Liberty inspired them with courage to oppose their breasts to the Hessian bayonet at Red Bank, and enabled them to endure with fortitude the cold and famine of Valley Forge."

" PRIMUS HALL, a native Bostonian, and long known to the citizens as a soap-boiler, served in the revolutionary war, and used to entertain the social circle with various anecdotes of his military experience ; among them an instance, where being himself in possession of a blanket, at a time when such a luxury had become scarce, Gen. WASHINGTON entered the tent, having appropriated his own bedding for the worn-out soldiers, HALL immediately tendered his blanket for the General, who replied, that he preferred sharing the privations with his fellow soldiers, and accordingly, Gen. WASHINGTON and PRIMUS HALL reposed for the night together."

The General did not then, Mr. Chairman, feel that instinctive horror; he knew nothing of that irreconcilable repugnance which

Colonizationists gravely affirm, is the natural consequence when the white man and his colored brother come in contact. George Washington, the most distinguished man of his time, and Primus Hall, negro soap-boiler! PAR NOBILE FRATRUM! Both reposing under the same blanket, and the moon still walked in her brightness, without blushing at the incongruous spectacle! Not a solitary star ceased its twinkling, in the deep blue vault of heaven!

"JOSHUA B. SMITH narrated to me 'that he was present at a company of distinguished Massachusetts men, when the conversation turned upon the exploits of Revolutionary times; and that the late Judge STORY related an instance of a Colored Artillerist who, while having charge of a cannon with a white fellow soldier, was wounded in one arm. He immediately turned to his comrade and proposed changing his position, exclaiming that he had yet one arm left, with which he could render some service to his country. The charge proved fatal to the heroic soldier, for another shot from the enemy killed him upon the spot. Judge STORY furnished other incidents of the bravery and devotion of Colored Soldiers, adding that he had often thought them and their descendants too much neglected considering the part they had sustained in the Wars; and he regretted that he did not, in early life, gather the facts into a shape for general information."

"In Rhode Island,' says Governor EUSTIS, in his able speech against Slavery in Missouri, 12th of twelfth month, 1820, 'the blacks formed an entire regiment, and they discharged their duty with zeal and fidelity. The gallant defence of Red Bank, in which the black regiment bore a part, is among the proofs of their valor.' In the contest it will be recollected that four hundred men met and repulsed, after a terrible and sanguinary struggle, fifteen hundred Hessian troops, headed by Count DONOP. The glory of the defence of Red Bank, which has been pronounced one of the most heroic actions of the War, belongs in reality to black men; yet who now hears them spoken of in connection with it? Among the traits which distinguished the black regiment, was devotion to their officers. In the attack made upon the American lines, near Croton river, on the 13th of fifth month, 1781, Colonel GREENE, the commander of the regiment, was cut down and mortally wounded; but the sabres of the enemy only reached him through the bodies of his faithful guard of blacks, who hovered over him to protect him, EVERY ONE OF WHOM WAS KILLED."

"Rev. DR. HARRIS, of Dunbarton, N. H., a revolutionary veteran stated in a speech at Francestown, N. H., some years ago, that on one occasion, the regiment to which he was attached was commanded to defend an important position which the enemy thrice assailed, and from which they were as often repulsed. 'There was,' said the venerable speaker, a Regiment of blacks in the same situation—a regiment of negroes fighting for our liberty and independence, not a white man among them but the officers—in the same dangerous and responsible position. Had they been unfaithful, or given way before the enemy, all would have been lost. Three times in succession were they attacked with most desperate fury by well-disciplined and veteran troops, and three times did they successfully repel the assault, and thus preserve an army. They fought thus through the war. They were brave and hardy troops."

"Dr. CLARKE, in the Convention which revised the Constitution of New York, in 1821, speaking of the Colored inhabitants of the State, said: 'My honorable colleague has told us that as the Colored people are not required to contribute to the protection or defence of the State, they are not entitled to an equal participation in the privileges of its citizens. But, Sir, whose fault is this? Have they ever refused to do military duty when called upon? It is haughtily asked, who will stand in the ranks shoulder to shoulder with a negro? I answer, no one in time of peace; no one when your musters and trainings are looked upon as mere pastimes; no one when your militia will shoulder their muskets and march to their trainings with as much unconcern as they would go to a sumptuous entertainment or a splendid ball. But, Sir, when the hour of danger approaches, your 'white' militia are just as willing that the man of Color should be set up as a mark to be shot at by the enemy, as to be set up themselves. In the War of the Revolution, these people helped to fight your battles by land and by sea. Some of your States were glad to turn out corps of Colored men, and to stand 'shoulder to shoulder' with them."

"In your late War, they contributed largely towards some of your most splendid victories. On Lakes Erie and Champlain where your fleets triumphed over a foe superior in numbers and engines of death, they were manned in a large proportion with men of Color. And in this very house, in the fall of 1814, a bill passed, receiving the approbation of all the branches of your Government, authorising the Governor to accept the services of a corps of two thousand of free people of Color. Sir, these were times which tried men's souls. In these times it was no sporting matter to bear arms. These were times when a man who shouldered his musket did not know but he bared his bosom to receive a death wound from the enemy ere he laid it aside; and in these times, these people were found as ready and as willing to volunteer in your service as any other. They were not compelled to go; they were not drafted. No; your pride had placed them beyond your compulsory power. But there was no necessity for its exercise; they were volunteers; yes, Sir, volunteers to defend that very country from the inroads and ravages of a ruthless and vindictive foe, which had treated them with insult, degradation, and Slavery."

"Volunteers are the best of Soldiers; give me the men, whatever be their complexion, that willingly volunteer, and not those who are compelled to turn out. Such men do not fight from necessity, nor from mercernary motives, but from principle."

"On the capture of WASHINGTON, by the British forces, it was judged expedient to fortify, without delay, the principal towns and cities exposed to similar attacks. The Vigilance Committee of Philadelphia waited upon three of the principal Colored citizens, namely, JAMES FORTEN, BISHOP ALLEN, and ABSALOM JONES, soliciting the aid of the people of Color in erecting suitable defence for the city. Accordingly, two thousand five hundred Colored men assembled in the State-House yard, and from thence marched to Gray's ferry, where they labored for two days, almost without intermission. Their labors were so faithful and efficient, that a vote of thanks was tendered them by the committee. A battalion of Colored troops were at the same time organized in the city, under an officer of the United States army; and they were on the point of marching to the frontier when peace was proclaimed."

On December 18, 1814, General JACKSON issued in the French language, the following address to the free people of Color: —

"SOLDIERS! — When on the banks of the Mobile I called you to take up arms, inviting you to partake the perils and glory of your *white fellow-citizens, I expected much from you*; for I was not ignorant that you possessed qualities most formidable to an invading enemy. I knew with what fortitude you could endure hunger and thirst, and all the fatigues of a campaign. *I knew well how you loved your native country*, and that you, as well as ourselves, had to defend what MAN holds most dear — his parents, wife, children, and property. YOU HAVE DONE MORE THAN I EXPECTED. In addition to the previous qualities I before knew you to possess, I found among you a noble enthusiasm, which leads to the performance of great things.

"Soldiers! The President of the United States shall hear how praiseworthy was your conduct in the hour of danger, and the representatives of the American people will give you the praise your exploits entitle you to. Your General, anticipates them in applauding your noble ardor.

"The enemy approaches; his vessels cover our lakes; our brave citizens are united, and all contention has ceased among them. Their only dispute is, who shall win the prize of valor, or who the most glory, its noblest reward. By Order,

THOMAS BUTLER, Aid-de-Camp."

But these quotations must suffice.

And, now, gentlemen, with the broad, blazing sunlight of the Revolution flashing across your souls, and revealing the prowess and patriotism of your colored citizens, in letters of such living brightness, will you, can you refuse the granting of this Petition? No, gentlemen, I see by the light of your eye, and the patriotic crimson that illumes your cheek, that you will report favorably upon this Petition.

This is professedly, a Republican government; we are an integral portion of this Republic. We claim the absolute right, the inalienable, God given right of Freemen. You, gentlemen, have no more right to say we shall not obtain a charter, than you have to monopolize the winds of heaven, or the rain which falls alike upon the just and the unjust. Because the sun hath looked more intensely upon me than on you, I, as a colored man, am doomed to degradation ; " hitherto shalt thou come and no further, and here shall thy proud waves be stayed." This is the imperious *dictum* that emanates from the *sanctum sanctorum* of Republican christianity, and Christian Republicanism.

But you might as well command the morning star to leap from its azure home, or command us what we shall eat and drink, or wherewithal we shall be clothed. It cannot be denied, that if we are men, we are entitled to all the rights of men every where; and no one has a right gentlemen, morally speaking, either natural or acquired, to dehumanize and segregate us from the rest of mankind. You may withold our right, but you can't annihilate it. The very word Right pre-supposes the idea of Obligation. The words are, in fact, reciprocal. We then, gentlemen, have the right ; where rests the obligation? It rests somewhere! Where; I ask, with increased emphasis, rests the obligation? I pause that you may reflect. But I will merely touch on another point, a point upon which, I suppose my learned friend, Robert Morris, Esq., will dwell at full length.

It has been affirmed, sir, that colored men cannot legally be enrolled among the General Militia; that we are among the absolute exempts. But this is an egregious error. What is the language of the Law, Sir, relative to enrollment, exemption, &c. Let us read the Third Section.

" Every able bodied white male citizen, resident in the Commonwealth, who is, or shall be of the age of 18, and under the age of 45 years, except persons enrolled in Volunteer Companies ; persons belonging

✻✻

to the religious denominations of Quakers, or Shakers, who shall procure to the assessors a certificate, as provided in the Second Section; idots, lunatics, common drunkards, vagabonds, paupers, and persons convicted of any infamous crimes in this, or any other State, shall be enrolled in the General Militia."

Now, gentlemen, who are the absolute exempts? Are the 65 gentlemen who have signed this Petition, embraced in the category? No, for the simple yet conclusive reason that they are not Quakers nor Shakers; (although the intonations of the thunder's voice, and the lurid lightnings of the wrath of man are sufficient to induce a general paralysis throughout our body-politic, and compel us to be Quakers and Shakers against our will;) we are not able to produce to the assessors a certificate, as provided in the second section, proving that we are idiots, or lunatics, or drunkards, common or uncommon, or vagabonds, or paupers, or persons convicted of any infamous crime. But gentlemen, although you do not place us in this honorable company by name, YET YOU VIRTUALLY "NUMBER US AMONG THE TRANGRESSORS."

Gentlemen, do we deserve to be placed in this category? If we do, we should be taken care of; for lunatics and idiots are not able to take care of themselves, and criminals should be looked after especially. If we do not, we have a right to demand that you withdraw us from the company with whom we find ourselves involuntarily associated. You will perceive that we are not literally among the absolute exempts, although prejudice may so construe it. For although able bodied white male citizens shall be enrolled among the general militia, there is nothing here which says able-bodied colored citizens shall NOT. It seems to be left optional with us. Our fathers were not able-bodied white male citizens; but they were able enough to face British cannon, in 1776 and 1812.

So, gentlemen, you perceive that we base our petition upon the grand, fundamental, eternal, Heaven-approving principle of RIGHT; OUR ABSOLUTE RIGHT TO ENJOY FULL CIVIL PRIVILEGES. If it can be proved we are not able-bodied MEN; if it can be proved we are incapable of performing every honorable duty, you should consider our petition as a gross insult to your body, but it not, there is no alternative but to treat us as citizens of this Commonwealth should be treated; as able-bodied, honorable men.

In the fourth and last place, Mr. Chairman, I WILL BRIEFLY NO-
TICE SOME OF THE BENEFICIAL RESULTS WHICH WILL ACCRUE
FROM THE GRANTING OF THIS PETITION.

And allow me to remark that these results will be reciprocally
beneficial. I am conscious, gentlemen, there are some men in the
country, foreigners especially, who would not sleep very soundly, unless your report were adverse to our Petition. There are some so
peculiarly sensitive, that were they to behold an able-bodied colored
company parading down State street, where fell the noble Crispus
Attucks, they would be almost ready to proclaim the hour of God's
judgment come; or, what is about the same thing in their estimation,
we would be upon the eve of a dissolution of the Union. They
would not shut their eyes, but to dream of miserable hobgoblins; and
black regiments of soldiers would so harrow up their little, narrow,
contracted souls, that with mournful and elongated visage they would
feel called on to walk up and down our streets, and proclaim, "Woe,
woe, woe" unto Massachusetts, and to the inhabitants thereof; "for
the great day of His wrath is come, and who shall be able to
stand?"

Why, gentlemen, if you grant us a charter, the soap bubble gas-
conade, and characteristic rhodomontade of Southern bullyism, would
be launched forth against you with fearful power. Think you South
Carolina would then stay in the Union, IF SHE COULD BY ANY
MEANS EXIST OUT OF IT?

But, Mr. Chairman, to be serious; if any one dreams of any evil
consequences inevitably flowing from the granting of this Petition,
we should charitably attribute all to the hallucination of a moon-
struck imagination. In the first place, grant our petition, and you
evince to the world, that Massachusetts careth for her colored citizens; that she does not repudiate them as vagrants or criminals, but
is disposed to help those who help themselves. It shews forth to the
world, that Massachusetts knows no man by the color of his skin, but
all, irrespective of accidental circumstances, stand upon one broad,
common, and ever enduring platform, on which the whole world may
stand and it will not fall.

We love Massachusetts; if she reciprocates that love, let her shew
forth her love by her works. Let her throw around us the mantle of
her protection, and then, O Massachusetts, if we forget thee, "may

our right hand forget its cunning, and our tongue cleave to the roof of our mouth." Yes! Let the old Bay State treat us as men, and she shall elicit our undying, indissoluble attachment. And neither height, nor depth, nor principalities, nor powers, nor things present, nor things to come, shall ever be able to alienate our affection from her. We will be with her in the sixth trouble, and in the seventh, we will neither leave nor forsake her. Amid the angry howling of the tempest, as well as in the cheering sunshine, we shall be ever found, a faithful few, indomitable, unterrified, who know their friends to love them. with that affection which nought but the Destroying Angel can annihilate.

Again, grant us this petition, and it will induce in us a determination to surmount every obstacle calculated to impede our progress ; to rise higher and *higher*, and HIGHER, until we scale the Mount of Heaven, and look down from our lofty and commanding position, upon our revilers and persecutors. Yes, sir ; it will incite us to renewed diligence, and cause our arid desert to rejoice and blossom as the rose. It will inspire us with confidence, and encourage us to hope amid the almost tangible darkness that envelopes us. We care not for the hoarse, rough thunder's voice, nor the lightning's lurid gleamings, if we are yet to be a people ; if we are yet to behold the superstructure of our liberties, consummated amid pæns of thanksgiving, and shouts from millions, redeemed, regenerated, and disenthralled.

You can to-day, gentlemen, either bid us hope on, hope ever, or contribute towards smothering those irrepressible aspirations after freedom which God has placed in our hearts, and stamped with His own eternity. Again, grant us our petition, and you shall be consoled with the reflection that you have done your duty; you shall elicit the approbation of Heaven, the admiration of every lover of truth, justice, and humanity. Yes, gentlemen, when Death, with his icy and attenuated fingers, shall begin to feel around your heart, your mind shall revert to the present hour, and the consciousness of having done your duty will send a thrill of joy through every avenue of your soul. It is needless, gentlemen, for me to exhort you to do your duty, regardless of the smiles and frowns of an ever-fluctuating public opinion. Finally, grant us our petition, and you perform a work upon which your children shall look with smiles of approval. I know a prophet has no honor in his own country. It is said, the evil that men do generally lives after them, while the good is often interred with their bones.

But I look down the vista of time, and I behold the faithful historian holding up to the gaze and admiration of the then living world as paragons of genuine philanthropy and pure patriotism, those who now elicit on every hand, the most virulent persecutions, the most vindictive anathemas; those who dare brave the storm ; who smile when the storm-cloud frowns ; and who, amid lightning, tempest, earthquake, whirlwind, dare proclaim, "OUR COUNTRY IS THE WORLD — OUR COUNTRYMEN, ALL MANKIND."

Gentlemen, will you show this day, that you are among the faithful few, and cause the wheels of the car of freedom to revolve with accelerated impetus. Our cause is onward. Our enemies might as well attempt to mesmerize an earthquake, or rock the whirlwind to sleep, or command the ocean, "Hitherto shalt thou come, and no farther," with the expectation of eliciting obedience to the mandate, as to attempt to crush the immortal aspirations of a people determined to be free.

Truth, Justice, Humanity, God, are on our side. They that are for us, are more than all that are against us. " *Magna est veritas, est prevalebet.*" " Lift up your eye foward the heavens; look also upon the earth ; the heavens shall vanish like smoke ; the earth shall be removed, and they that dwell therein shall die; but my salvation shall be forever, and my righteousness shall not be abolished." Thus saith the Lord. " Let the rains descend, and the winds blow, and the floods come, and beat upon this house ; it shall stand, being founded upon a rock."

And now, Mr. Chairman, I have done. Pardon me for trespassing so long upon your kind indulgence. I hope I have not spoken in vain. May you discharge your duty to your God, to yourselves, and to bleeding humanity, and ultimately attain to light, life and immortality.